CHORAL DIRECTOR'S REHEARSAL AND PERFORMANCE GUIDE

Lewis Gordon

PARKER PUBLISHING COMPANY
West Nyack, New York 10995

10 9 8 7 6 5 4 3 2

Most of the illustrations have been taken from *Choral Director's Complete Handbook*, Lewis Gordon,
© 1977, published by Parker Publishing Company, Inc., West Nyack, New York. Used by permission
of the publisher.

Library of Congress Cataloging-in-Publication Data

Gordon, Lewis, [date]
    Choral director's rehearsal and performance guide / Lewis Gordon.
        p.   cm.
    Includes index.
    ISBN 0-13-133398-4
    1. Conducting, Choral.   2. Choirs (Music)   3. Choral singing-
-Instruction and study.   I. Title.
MT85.G74   1989   89-8831
782.5′145—dc20   CIP
                                                         MN

ISBN 0-13-133398-4

PARKER PUBLISHING COMPANY
BUSINESS & PROFESSIONAL DIVISION
A division of Simon & Schuster
West Nyack, New York 10995

Printed in the United States of America

ABOUT THIS GUIDE

The purpose of the *Choral Director's Rehearsal and Performance Guide* is to give you practical suggestions and solutions for establishing and developing a quality choral program in any school, church, or community setting. It provides a unique compendium of concepts and ideas for planning, organizing, executing, and evaluating rehearsal and performance activities.

Included is basic as well as more advanced information for all choral directors. New directors will find guidelines and procedures presented in a logical sequence—to assist them in building their first choral program from preliminary planning to guiding singers through performances. More seasoned leaders will find advanced conducting techniques as well as insights based on thirty years of personal experience and dialogue with successful conductors.

The *Guide* deals with some of the more challenging issues facing today's vocal ensemble leaders, including:

- How can you size up your choral situation in terms of the group itself, the rehearsal facility, the repertoire, and funding? Chapter 1, "Surveying the Choral Program," discusses these and other considerations.

- What role should popular taste and public entertainment play in the selection of repertoire? Chapter 2, "Laying the Foundation," offers perspectives.

- What kind of reputation do you have as a businessperson? Chapter 3, "Managing the Program," details specifics for establishing and managing your choral program.

- Do you use proper body posture when conducting? Chapter 4, "Establishing Rudiments of Conducting," outlines the components of correct posture as well as the basic conducting patterns.

- What skills are needed to combine chorus with orchestra? Chapter 5, "Developing Expressive Conducting Techniques," provides suggestions for working with instrumentalists.

- Do your rehearsals follow a logical sequence? Find out about rehearsal preparation, execution, and culmination in Chapter 6, "Conducting Rehearsals."

- How do you motivate your choral groups in both rehearsals and performances? Guidelines are given in Chapter 7, "Motivating the Ensemble."

- What skills do you need to achieve a superior choral sound? Chapter 8, "Working With Singers," acquaints you with the mechanics of singing and offers exercises for working with groups and individuals.

- How do you get an amateur choir to perform an avant garde work with conviction? Concepts are discussed in Chapter 9, "Developing Authentic Style."

- How do you "teach music" varying widely from "serious" to "light"? Strategies based on recent research are presented in Chapter 10, "Learning Music."

- How do you begin the refinement process that's needed for a concert performance? Chapter 11, "Polishing and Interpreting Music," offers suggestions for improving choral diction, coordinating the ensemble, and developing expressivity.

- What technical resources should you consider for having the best possible choral performance? Chapter 12, "Preparing for Performance," suggests guidelines.

- Does concert performance success equate with overall choral program success? Chapter 13, "Evaluating the Choral Program and Its Participants," suggests methods for assessment.

In short, the *Choral Director's Rehearsal and Performance Guide* provides a comprehensive source of ideas and concepts necessary to bring your choral program up to maximum effectiveness. Checklists and charts are provided for direct access to important topics. Examples, illustrations, and situations based on actual experiences are included for clarification. I hope all this information will help you and your choral groups have one successful performance after another!

Lewis Gordon

ABOUT THE AUTHOR

Dr. Lewis Gordon is Professor of Fine and Performing Arts at Saint Joseph's University. He is also choral director at Villanova University, whose ensembles he has lead in performances throughout the eastern United States and in Ireland.

Previously he taught music at Mount Union College in Ohio where his Concert Choir was selected to perform several world premieres at the 1981 College Music Society National Convention.

From 1977 to 1980, Lewis Gordon was choral director at Stockton State College in New Jersey. While there he toured Poland with the Stockton Chorale under the auspices of the Friendship Ambassadors Foundation.

Dr. Gordon is a graduate of The Juilliard School where he studied choral conducting with Abraham Kaplan and voice with Jennie Tourel. In 1980 he completed his Doctorate of Musical Arts at Temple University.

Lewis Gordon is author of *Choral Director's Complete Handbook*, published by Parker Publishing Company. He is also a tenor soloist, performing actively in concerts and recitals.

CONTENTS

CHAPTER 1

SURVEYING THE CHORAL PROGRAM

A surveyor inspects a tract of land to determine its location, boundaries, and features. Choral directors also need to "get a lay of the land" when establishing and developing their vocal programs. Quite often it's even a good idea to conduct a "self survey," to weigh one's own strengths and weaknesses against a new or existing choral position.

The profession of choral directing can be a risky business. It's one thing to possess musical talent and skill; it's quite another to be really *effective* within a given situation. Vocal ensembles, like their directors, have distinct personalities. Some traits are changeable; others "come with the territory." Here are two important points to keep in mind when considering a new choral position.

- Regardless of differences between the director and the group, there must be a basis for compatibility if success is to occur.

- When a conductor grabs at an opportunity without regard to compatibility, choice may be doomed to failure.

DIRECTOR, KNOW THYSELF!

The following statements were made by two eminently successful choral directors:

I have never heard in any rehearsal such snafued enunciation or such careless, perverse, and dispirited rhythm.[1]

Under no circumstances should the conductor display any impatience even when things do not go as well as they should.[2]

---

[1]Shaw letter quoted in Joseph A. Mussulman, *Dear People . . . Robert Shaw* (Bloomington: Indiana University Press, 1979), p. 51.

[2]Kurt Thomas, *The Choral Conductor*, English adaptation by Alfred Mann and William H. Reese. (New York: Associated Music Publishers, 1971), p. 76.

PERSONALITY INVENTORY

Where would you place yourself along each of the following continua? Are you *both* extremes in any category? If so, when does one trait take over from the other?

Talker	Do'er
Artistic	Intellectual
Persuasive	Facilitative
Worrier	Hedonist
Docile	Easily Angered
Gregarious	Loner
Intimidator	Charmer
Relaxed	Intense
Organizer	Planner
Humorous	Serious
Anxious	Confident
Decisive	Vascillating
Lazy	Industrious

Figure 1–1

Both musicians were able to achieve superior results with their ensembles. Yet each learned how to work effectively utilizing his own personal leadership style.

Before accepting a choral position, it's always a good idea to take a look at yourself to determine your strengths and weaknesses. What kind of personality do you have? How well will you relate to the choral ensemble? It to you? A *Personality Inventory* is a good place to begin your quest to "know thyself" (Figure 1–1). Here's an actual example which demonstrates the importance of this topic. (Situation 1–A.)

SITUATION 1–A

John A. was a successful, charming conductor who depended on friendly persuasion for results. When he took over a new choir, his singers complained, "he's too easy . . . he's too nice." The former director was a tyrant who had intimidated (and indoctrinated) the

ensemble with his authoritarian approach. Eventually John left the
position in search for a more compatible situation.

This discussion is not intended to suggest that we cannot improve our-
selves nor to suggest that a choral ensemble's attitudes cannot be changed.
But it is important that we balance our dreams and ambitions with a perspective about who we really are and what we can hope to accomplish.

MAKING PRELIMINARY ESTIMATES

Before accepting a new position as choral director, you will need to take a
careful look at the organization as it stands. If this will be a new ensemble,
you should determine as best you can its potential for success. For example,
will administrative and financial support be adequate?

If the group is established, it might be helpful to know something about
its traditions, its successes, and its failures. Why did the former director
leave? (See Situation 1–B.)

SITUATION 1–B

The principal of a high school was committed to excellence in sports
and supportive of the marching band. He viewed the choral program
as a social and therapeutic activity. The choral director attempted for
five years to get his decrepit rehearsal room painted. He resigned
last year to take another position.

Use the following checklist to size up your new choral situation:

1. *The Choral Group*

- Type of group: church, school, community
- Configuration of the ensemble: SA, TB, SAB, SATB
- Size of the group: chamber, mid-size, large
- Member selection: non-auditioned, competitive, volunteer, profes-
  sional
- Rehearsal schedule: when, length of rehearsals

- Attendance policy: in effect, actual practice
- Concert schedule: when, types, where
- Group strengths and weaknesses: music learning, level of performance, balance between vocal sections

2. *The Singers*

- Ages: children, high school, college, adult, combinations
- Level of ability: previous choral experience, voice lessons, soloists, instrumental instruction
- Values: sense of purpose, level of achievement, likes and dislikes

3. *The Rehearsal Facility*

- Location: convenience, conflicts in usage
- Characteristics: size, acoustics, lighting, heating, ventilation, lines of sight
- Equipment: piano, chairs, music stand, chalkboard, stereo equipment, music and wardrobe storage

4. *Repertoire*

- Music on file: styles, genres, purchasing trends, numbers of copies
- Recent concerts: choices of music, level of difficulty, use of instruments, performances with other groups

5. *The Market*

- Potential singers: size of population, level of interest, recent trends in ensemble participation
- Concert attendance: number of concertgoers, extent of publicity
- Ensemble image: name of group, type of wardrobe, level of esteem

6. *Funding*

- Current budget: source of funds, allocations
- Potential needs: payment of musicians, purchase of music, printing costs, wardrobe, incidentals

7. *Key Personnel*

- Accompanist: volunteer or professional, returning or new, abilities and limitations
- Officers: figureheads or crucial workers, duties

8. *Administrative Considerations*

- Calendar year restrictions: holidays, seasonal religious requirements, conflicting events
- Other organizations: involvement of singers with other activities, conflicting schedules

CLARIFYING THE ENSEMBLE'S ROLE

Quite often, the major role of a vocal ensemble is predetermined by certain permanent conditions. The following examples illustrate this point:

- A new church expects its budding choir to sing an anthem every Sunday.
- Members of an ethnic chorus usually meet for the purpose of performing music from their culture.

Yet, even when a vocal organization's main purpose seems evident to the conductor, confusion may exist among its members. According to Royal Stanton,

> Choirs in other-than-professional settings are comprised primarily of musical laymen, young and old. They participate for many reasons: as part of a learning process, for recreation, musical satisfaction, personal accomplishment, to be of service, in response to their inner need to be part of a group, or from mere curiosity.[3]

After clearly defining the role of the ensemble, you as director must set a unified course of action for the entire group. Figure 1–2 presents factors which tend to control or at least influence a choral group's basic nature.

---

[3]Royal Stanton, *The Dynamic Choral Conductor* (Delaware Water Gap: Shawnee Press, 1971), p. 3.

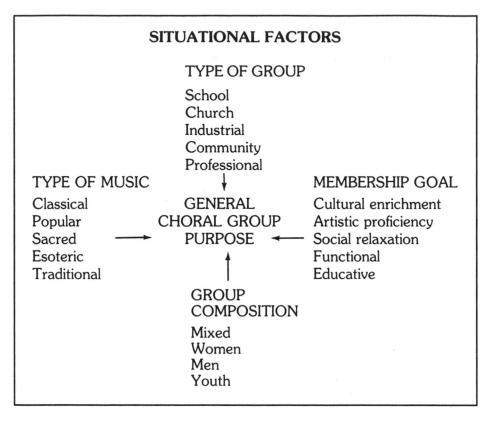

SITUATIONAL FACTORS

Figure 1–2

Sometimes, the role of an ensemble may shift. I once took over a socially oriented, informal singing group, then saw it evolve into a performance-oriented concert choir. Ask yourself the following questions when attempting to define your ensemble's role:

1. *How precisely can I pinpoint the organization's role?* For example, if this is a school group, is its main purpose to educate its members, the audience, or both? If a church choir, should it perform texts taken from the daily gospel, or provide a more general sacred ambience for the service? (See Situation 1–C.)

2. *What impact should my singers' interests have on the ensemble's role?* Shall they "sing for themselves" by performing esoteric music or "reach out to their audience" by performing flashy hits?

3. *Does the organization have more than one role?* Will your school

chorus perform benefit concerts to aid muscular dystrophy? Does your church choir perform on a European tour every three years?

SITUATION 1–C

Joe H. was determined to perform "masterworks of sacred literature" every Sunday with his church choir. Unfortunately, his choir was lacking in number and ability. The congregation found the performances to be uninspiring, and the choir began losing members.

CHOOSING SINGERS

Undoubtedly, the most crucial aspect of building a choral program is locating new members. Without singers there will be no choir, and without the best available performers the organization can't reach its true potential.

Selling the Program

The extent of your "marketing campaign" will vary. For a well-established popular community group, a single announcement in the local newspaper may be sufficient to produce a healthy response. For a new group in the process of building its image, several avenues of communication may be necessary to reach interested singers. Some possibilities include:

- Posters
- Public announcements in classes, at meetings, in dining halls, etc.
- Mailed notices
- Radio announcements
- Word of mouth through members
- Audition information provided within printed programs
- Information desks at busy locations

The actual information you choose to provide these potential singers, as well as the way in which it is presented, is very important because, in effect, you are attempting to "sell" the choral program. Obviously, such basic facts as the time and place for auditions need to be stated, but other appealing information should be included. Some comment about an exciting choral work to be performed or an interesting upcoming performance is always helpful. (Figure 1–3.)

JOIN THE COLBY-SAWYER CONCERT CHOIR!

Sing with the Dartmouth Glee Club

*   *   *   *   *

Travel to Boston and perform in historic Old North Church

AUDITIONS FOR NEW MEMBERS

Tuesday, February 18 and Wednesday, February 19

7–9 p.m.   *   Gordon Hall   *   Sawyer Center

Figure 1–3

Why Audition?

Some volunteer ensembles traditionally accept singers without requiring an audition. For example, many high schools require that their "Freshman Chorus" be open without qualification to any student willing to attend on a regular basis. The word "audition" or "try-out" does seem to conjure up feelings of anxiety among prospective members and may even scare some of them away. On the other hand, auditions sometimes generate a sense of pride and accomplishment among accepted singers. Auditions can be helpful for the following reasons:

- Determine range for assignment to proper vocal section
- Serve as a basis for judging vocal quality and musicianship
- Get to know auditioner's background, health, and personality
- Diagnose vocal strengths and shortcomings

- Determine seating for strong, weak, and complementary voices
- Choose soloists
- Establish standards of acceptance for select groups

One solution for avoiding "pre-selection jitters" is to defer the audition. After a "get-acquainted" or probationary period, hold a delayed tryout. Choose a day for each vocal section, then have individual members sing for you.

Setting Up Auditions

Will your audition session reveal what prospective singers *can* do—or what they *can't* do? Long lines and unanswered questions cause anxious, disgruntled singers; smooth-running procedures and human sensitivity pave the way for maximum responsiveness. Here are five suggestions to help ensure successful auditions.

1. *Hold a general meeting before auditions.* The audition procedure can be explained, followed by a brief demonstration. Perhaps you will choose to warm up the entire group. Rehearsal and concert schedules can also be discussed during the meeting.

2. *Hold auditions privately.* This helps to alleviate nervousness and allows for a more personalized audition. For large numbers of singers, use an assistant to facilitate a smooth flow of individuals in and out of the audition room. Make sure your helper knows enough about the choral program to answer questions effectively.

3. *Set up a schedule.* If you hold a general meeting, times may be assigned in advance. Another solution is to provide time cards. Those with later times may leave and return.

4. *Provide a "fact sheet" to be read before the audition.* Besides rehearsal and concert schedules, information could include rules and regulations, repertoire to be performed, general facts about the ensemble, course credits, and fees.

5. *Use an audition form.* Before singers enter the audition, have them complete their part of an audition form. Cards work better than paper for handling and later filing. Figure 1–4 presents a typical format. A comprehensive form will include sections to record information about biography, previous musical experience, the audition itself, and decisions regarding acceptance and assignment.

AUDITION FORM

STOCKTON STATE COLLEGE SINGERS

* * * * * *

INFORMATION FORM

* * * * * * * *

Name _____ Class _____
       Last   First

Dorm or Local Address _____
_____ Telephone No. _____

Previous Choir Experience _____
_____

Soloist Experience _____
List any instruments you play. How well? _____
_____

Other Current Organizations _____
_____

Name and Location of H.S. Attended _____
_____

Side 1

Range   Vocal Assignment _____

Quality _____   Section Leader _____
Intonation _____   Soloist _____
Melodic Retention _____   Accompanist _____
Rhythmic Retention _____   Instrumentalist _____
Sight Reading _____

Comments:

Side 2

Figure 1–4

Determining Audition Procedures

The actual audition may range from simply having the singer perform a short song or sing several scales to administering intensive diagnostic tests in musical memory and sight reading. The choice of components will be based on two important factors.

1. *Level of selectivity.* How critical will you be when choosing new choir members? A small school with several conflicting activities might require you to choose a low level of selectivity and to "take what you can get." Conversely, a semi-professional chamber ensemble would require fairly selective auditions.

With large turnouts of singers, time can be saved by holding *two* auditions. The first serves the purpose of quickly screening candidates for those with superior qualifications. The second audition is more selective.

2. *Criteria for examination.* After deciding on the level of selectivity, you must consider exactly what it is you hope to discover about the auditioner. If the standards for acceptance into the vocal organization are minimal, you would probably only be interested in finding out if the individual can "carry a tune." You would also need to know the vocal range for assignment to the proper section. (Figure 1–5.) On the other hand, high selectivity would require you to consider such details as vocal agility and enunciation.

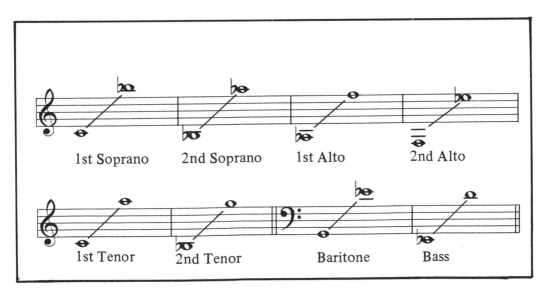

Figure 1–5

Sometimes the most talented singer or the best sight reader turns out to be a mediocre ensemble member. Experienced choral leaders often discover that individuals with strong interest and dedication accomplish more for a group than others with more musical ability. Consider such factors as personality, attitude, and alertness during the audition. Figure 1–6 presents a comprehensive list of criteria for examination along with desirable characteristics and potential problems for each item. (See Situation 1–D.)

THE AUDITION: CRITERIA FOR EXAMINATION

VOCAL

Criteria	Desirable Characteristics	Potential Problems
Range	Capable of performing extremes necessary for vocal part	Undue strain at top; insufficient volume at bottom
	Tessitura comfortable for vocal part	Gaps or breaks Undue heaviness or weightiness
Tone Quality	Clear, capable of blending	Nasal, protruding
	Color rich and vibrant	Breathy and unfocused
Control	Agile, capable of performing fast tempos	Unwieldy, sluggish
	Steady, pleasant vibrato	Excessive wobble; strained straight tone
	Sustained phrasing	Unsupported; breath-ridden phrasing
	Latitude of volume, ability to sustain; smooth **crescendi** and **decrescendi**	Limited volume; unsteady
Intonation	Ability to attack on pitch, then maintain	Swooping; continual sharping and flatting

| Diction | Proper pronunciation and enunciation | Muddy or faulty vowels and consonants Unusual dialect |

MUSICIANSHIP

Criteria	*Desirable Characteristics*	*Potential Problems*
Musical memory	Ability to remember melodic passages and rhythmic figures	Inability to discern patterns of sound
Sight reading	Ability to perform melodic profiles	No sense of key or intervals
	Ability to perform rhythmic patterns	No sense of meter or duration

GENERAL

Criteria	*Desirable Characteristics*	*Potential Problems*
Personality	Enthusiastic; confident	Lethargic; anxious
Attitude	Seriousness of purpose; cooperative	Flippant; know-it-all
Other Activities	No conflicts with ensemble schedule	Low academic average; excessive participation

Figure 1–6

SITUATION 1–D

Henry R. chose singers on the basis of sight-reading proficiency. The ensemble always seemed to "bog down" in its ability to learn music. Then, he began choosing on the basis of musical memory tests. Intonation and choral repertoire learning improved considerably.

Constructing an Audition Test

Devising a format for auditioning is a highly personal task based on past experiences and general knowledge about the singers. For purposes of expediency, tryouts usually do not exceed ten minutes. Here is a lengthy procedure which could be used to conduct a thorough, comprehensive audition.

1. Review the audition form with the singer. Try to gain some perspective about the individual's experience, personality, and attitude.

2. Vocalize the auditioner down a five-note scale passage, modulating each exercise downward until the lowest comfortable note is reached. Reverse this process by vocalizing upward until the highest comfortable note is reached. Note range, tessitura, and any unusual characteristics of the voice.

3. Have the auditioner perform a well-known song. Play only harmonic accompaniment to see if he or she can sustain the melodic line. Listen for vocal quality. Ask the singer to perform the song again emphasizing words and interpretation. Listen for diction and musicianship.

4. Have the auditioner perform a rapidly moving exercise in a comfortable key. (See Figure 1–7 for an example.) Repeat the exercise if necessary. Listen for vocal agility and intonation.

5. Have the auditioner perform a sustained exercise which incorporates dynamic latitude. (See Figure 1–8.) Listen for vibrato and volume control.

6. Play musical memory exercises, one at a time, in sequence and ask auditioner to sing them back (Figure 1–9). Note singer's ability to remember melody and rhythm.

7. Have the auditioner sight read from exercises graduated in difficulty (Figure 1–10.) Play beginning note only.

Figure 1–7

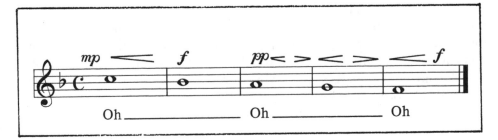

Figure 1–8

Figure 1–9

Figure 1–10

8. Have the auditioner sight read his or her voice part in unknown four-part songs (perhaps composed by you). These should be graduated in difficulty and accompanied (excluding the singer's part) so that the part can be heard contextually. If he or she stumbles, allow a second chance to see if mistakes are corrected. As an alternative approach, have the other three parts performed by other members of a vocal quartet.

CHAPTER 2

LAYING THE FOUNDATION

Quality choral programs have a sense of purpose. Rehearsals are characterized by steady growth and achievement as singers move closer to concert goals. Each encounter with repertoire results in new insights and improved performance. Choral programs without a sense of purpose flounder. Rehearsals are marred by aimlessness, and members seem to have an "identity crisis" with their ensemble.

The success of your choral program will be largely determined by your ability to set goals and then organize purposeful activities. The captain of a ship spends considerable time charting its course. I know reputable choral directors who spend as much time planning and choosing music as they spend in rehearsals.

SETTING GOALS

The choral program is primarily a performance-oriented activity. In his book, *Choral Music Education*, Paul Roe contends "a choir must perform as frequently as it can concertize with polish and finesse."[1]

To a large extent, concerts serve as yardsticks for measuring an ensemble's level of achievement, and standards are met when your singers reach pre-established goals. For example, you may choose to improve vibrancy in pianissimo singing and select several "mood pieces" as vehicles for achieving your desired results.

Yet good directors have always been concerned with more than technically proficient performances. As educators we hope to improve musicianship; as humanists, we are concerned about individual needs and social development. Figure 2–1 suggests several areas of development necessary to ensure a well-balanced choral program.

The establishment of goals within each area of development is an ongoing concern. As cycles are completed, the ensemble as a whole moves through a series of stages or levels.

---

[1]Paul F. Roe, *Choral Music Education* (Englewood Cliffs: Prentice-Hall, 1970), p. 328.

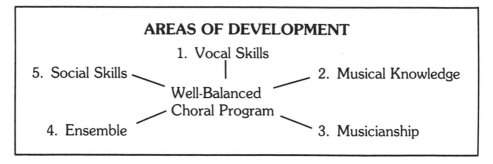

AREAS OF DEVELOPMENT

1. Vocal Skills

5. Social Skills · ~ Well-Balanced · 2. Musical Knowledge
Choral Program

4. Ensemble · 3. Musicianship

Figure 2–1

Achievement Levels

Vocal ensembles tend to fall into one of three achievement levels depending on their current stage of development. These levels are presented below together with suggested types of goals suitable for each area of development. Your final selection of goals will be based on the uniqueness of your choral program.

Achievement Level I: Orientation. In this initial phase individuals "learn the ropes" of the organization. Some plausible goals are:

- Vocal Skills: Introduction to warm-up exercises; accurate vowel production
- Musical Knowledge: Identification of basic musical terms; familiarity with score mechanics
- Musicianship: Competency in sight-reading; identifying similar and contrasting tonal patterns
- Ensemble: Individual sensitivity to balance and blend within sections; precision in attacks and releases
- Social Skills: Familiarity with organizational policies and procedures; adjustment to new director

Achievement Level II: Growth. Members learn to contribute more effectively through improved music-learning skills and qualitative singing. Teamwork is emphasized.

- Vocal Skills: Ranges extended; greater control of dynamics
- Musical Knowledge: Perception of forms; identification of harmonies

- Musicianship: Sense for adapting proper articulation such as legato or staccato; phrasing without obtrusive breathing
- Ensemble: Sectional sensitivity to balance and blend between sections; adjustment of intonation
- Social Skills: Empathic response to group concerns; sense of belonging

Achievement Level III: Culmination. Skills become more refined with emphasis on interpretation and expressivity.

- Vocal Skills: Development of various vocal colors; improved resonation
- Musical Knowledge: Identification of types of compositions; understanding historical and stylistic relationships
- Musicianship: Ability to arch phrases; sensitivity to rubato
- Ensemble: Interplay between sections; active nonverbal communication between performers
- Social Skills: Sense of commitment to group; willingness to sacrifice and endure

The wise choral director estimates the ensemble's present achievement level, then establishes new goals for each area of development. Here are some factors to keep in mind when planning.

1. New ensembles comprised of singers with little or no previous experience may require three or more years to reach Achievement Level III.
2. The pace of achievement will be largely determined by the status of the majority. A few new members usually "catch up" with an established group; a "bumper crop" of new singers will slow progress.
3. Choral groups with high membership turnover may be forced to go backwards at the beginning of each year.
4. Ensembles with limited potential for development may have difficulty reaching Achievement Level III. Factors such as talent and degree of selectivity will ultimately determine how far the group can go.

PLANNING PERFORMANCES

Nothing beats performances for motivation. These special events serve as catalysts for energizing singers' efforts. In a healthy organization they may be viewed as milestones in achievement.

Choral ensembles usually have their share of traditional or "required" concerts such as the Sunday church service or the annual spring concert. School choruses often are expected to participate in assemblies and graduation ceremonies. However, new and unique experiences await those willing to move beyond the usual "in-house" concerts. My community male chorus recently performed for a capacity audience at a large air force base and was transported to and from the concert by military airplane. (See Situation 2–A.)

SITUATION 2–A

Sylvia M. was preparing her ensemble for a concert tour in Poland. She contacted a local, predominantly Polish, Catholic church about the possibility of performing there. The response was overwhelming. After the concert, the choristers were greeted with speeches, gifts, and a farewell dinner.

Locating additional performance outlets requires hard work and perseverance. Here are some places to begin your search. I have included personal observations for your consideration.

Festivals and shared concerts. These are great for first appearances with a new group because of relatively short performance time requirements. When ensembles combine for a finale, the experience can be exhilarating. Problems may occur when ensembles are mismatched in style or level of achievement.

Competitions. They can provide incentive for raising standards of performance, especially when objective, constructive critiques are provided. Sometimes the pressure of contests results in dissatisfaction and excessive rivalry. Choirs "hungry for victory" may become preoccupied with technical proficiency and lose sight of other values.

Conventions and annual meetings. These events provide an opportunity to "showcase" your vocal group. Convention hotels are occasionally in need of quality local entertainment. Why not get a list of upcoming events, then contact the sponsoring organizations directly? Make sure that performance facilities are adequate. Pianos are notoriously abused and often out of tune.

Places of worship. Sometimes churches and synagogues provide an architectural ambience unmatched by concert halls. Participation within a service or Mass will require careful choice of sacred music; many congregations also hold social activities and would welcome secular music. Appropriateness and taste are prime considerations in your choice of repertoire. For example, you may wish to avoid drinking songs.

Television and radio appearances. Local networks are especially on the lookout for choral groups at Christmas time. Pre-taped productions allow your singers to see and/or hear themselves. However, studios are usually acoustically dry and unflattering to voices. Bright lights also cause excessive heat and can turn a recording session into a tedious process.

Community celebrations. Town officials sometimes invite musical ensembles to enhance special events such as Memorial Day. Check local newspapers for upcoming activities and have several patriotic selections "ready to go." If held outdoors, you will need to consider amplification of your singers. Watch out for rain!

Social and service clubs. Members often combine dining with entertainment. Insist that your ensemble perform after the meal. Otherwise, your contribution may be lost in the banter of conversation and the din of clattering dishes.

Shopping malls. Appearances can provide excellent publicity for your upcoming formal concert. But, unless chairs are provided, you will be confronted by constant noise and audience migration.

Hospitals and retirement homes. Veterans Administration hospitals often run a busy concert schedule for their patients and provide good performance facilities. Audiences are always appreciative.

Matching the Ensemble with the Performance

The final decision whether or not to accept a performance should be based on compatibility. A *collegium musicum* will not be well received at a football game. Before accepting an invitation, make sure you can answer the following questions:

- Who will sponsor the concert?
- Where and when will the performance take place?
- What kinds of expenses or financial arrangements are involved?
- What kind of facilities, equipment, and musical instruments will be available?
- Who will attend the concert?
- How large an audience is expected?
- What type of music will they expect?

- How long will the concert be?
- What achievement level will be appropriate?

Sometimes performance requirements may be too demanding. Last year I turned down a request to have my university chorus perform in an opera. Long rehearsal hours necessitated by staging would have cut into preparation for our spring concert tour. On the other hand, ensembles may be "over-qualified" for a particular situation. Would you expect the Mormon Tabernacle Choir to perform for Molly Pott's tea party? Consider the value of the concert experience to your singers when deciding whether to accept or reject a performance. (See Situation 2–B.)

SITUATION 2–B

Bruce W.'s glee club accepted an offer to perform after dinner at a nearby country club. The club manager acted surprised when the choral director introduced his accompanist three days before the concert. The country club had no piano.

Setting Up the Concert Season

Planning musical events for an entire year requires foresight and attention to detail. For example, what would happen to your school vocal group if you scheduled its last performance of the season in March? Several important coordinating factors should be considered when you prepare long-range concert schedules.

Potential conflicts. Planning a community choral concert on the night of a local election could result in a complete flop. Note all important events which have already been scheduled, and then try to work around them.

Spacing. Make sure groups of concerts and tours are spread throughout the entire year. If you are planning a cluster of concerts, as in a tour, allow for sufficient "recuperation time" between performances.

Variety. It might be fun singing school songs at an important pep rally, but appearing every week could become boring.

Repertoire demands. The local businessmen's club may want your group to perform two days after the annual Christmas concert—and most of them will be there too! Will you need new repertoire?

The Planning Calendar

Listing the dates and times of upcoming concerts is one way to keep track of events. Calendars, however, offer a better perspective because they clearly reveal the time *between* concerts. And, as we know, directors see these intervening periods as valuable rehearsal time. Calendars with write-in space for each date work best. Here are two further suggestions which I have found to work particularly well

- Align small monthly calendars side by side and paste on a cardboard backing. This will provide you with the "big picture."
- For weekly church planning, cut horizontal slits within each Sunday calendar square. Cut small cards which will slide halfway into these slits. Print proposed anthems on the cards, then move them around to get variety.

Computing Rehearsal Time

Assessing the total hours necessary to learn and perform repertoire for an entire program is a difficult task. Sometimes factors such as unusually high absence slow down progress, and time estimates must be continually revised. The only way to compute required rehearsal time is to have an intimate knowledge of your ensemble's capabilities and then to analyze each musical work by the following criteria:

- Length of the work
- Level of note-learning difficulty
- Level of technical difficulty
- Level of interpretive difficulty
- Special coordinating problems (use of additional instruments or divided choirs)
- Memorization time (if applicable)

At this point I find it useful to plan blocks of rehearsals according to three stages of repertoire development.

- Note learning and technical mastery
- Polishing
- Interpreting

This approach allows the choral ensemble the opportunity to develop its repertoire as a composite, organic unit. More variety in rehearsals is also achieved by moving from work to work within each stage.

SELECTING MUSIC

Music is best chosen after development goals have been determined and performance requirements established. The importance of making wise choices cannot be overemphasized. According to Gordon Lamb in his book, *Choral Techniques,* "the selection of repertoire is probably the most demanding and time-consuming task facing a choral director."[2]

Repertoire must be selected with perspective and balance. Conductors who choose exclusively on the basis of self-interest or personal whim run the risk of losing their singers and audiences. In a sense, repertoire selection is a juggling act in which several ingredients for success are balanced. (See Figure 2–2.)

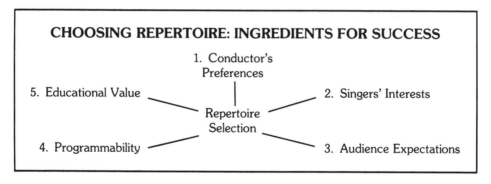

CHOOSING REPERTOIRE: INGREDIENTS FOR SUCCESS

1. Conductor's Preferences

5. Educational Value

Repertoire Selection

2. Singers' Interests

4. Programmability

3. Audience Expectations

Figure 2–2

Each of these factors is discussed below. The degree of emphasis will depend on your personal choral situation. For example, church choir directors place a high priority on programmability when they consider anthems appropriate for a particular service.

1. *Conductor's preferences.* A choral ensemble is sensitive to its conductor's likes and dislikes. If its leader feels no enthusiasm for a particular work, how can a vocal group find interest? On the other hand, directors with limited repertoire palettes hold back enterprising ensembles. Quality exam-

[2]Gordon H. Lamb, *Choral Techniques,* 2nd ed. (Dubuque: William C. Brown, 1979), p. 95.

ples can be found within almost every category and style of music. Attending others' concerts, participating in music reading sessions, and visiting music stores leads to fresh, viable repertoire selection.

2. *Singers' interests.* Younger performers tend to favor popular music. The upsurge of jazz and show choirs since the 1960s has led to an outpouring of contemporary repertoire of varied quality. Can you discern the difference between artistic craftsmanship and faddish insignificance?

Comprehensive choral programs provide opportunities to experience traditional and classical styles as well. You must find ways to convince younger singers that works which seem to lack immediate surface appeal may prove to be enjoyable and enriching.

3. *Audience expectations.* Concertgoers are preconditioned by the type of event they plan to attend. Your choir's performance of Handel's *Ode on the Death of Queen Caroline* might incur an unusual response at a festive banquet!

Sometimes parents and friends reluctantly attend concerts because someone they love participates. How can you "bridge the gap" and "turn them on" to your group's efforts?—By choosing works rich in expression and vitality; by captivating them through exciting performance.

4. *Programmability.* Unless you plan with forethought, your repertoire selections may end up in curious juxtapositions at concert time. Choose "blocks" of music which fit together and complement each other. For example, if you decide to concentrate on Renaissance motets, consider alternating fast with slow examples.

5. *Educational value.* The developmental goals and achievement levels cited earlier in this chapter are attained through careful selection of repertoire. For example, if your singers need to improve intonation, you may decide to "fight fire with fire" by choosing several *a cappella* selections. Many school directors plan a two- or three-year "repertoire cycle" enabling their students to become familiar with music from all historical periods.

Guidelines for Choosing Repertoire

After weighing the relative importance of the abovementioned factors, you are ready to begin the actual selection process with informed perspective and balance. The following guidelines should be considered when making choices:

1. *Choose music of aesthetic value.* Identifying artistic value in choral music is a process which can be undertaken by anyone willing to question

rather than blindly accept a work's potential value. The following questions are useful when you are attempting to determine aesthetic content:

- Is this work composed with craftsmanship? Compositional technique, regardless of style, should be permeated by quality of workmanship.
- Is this work significant? Significance implies a sense of durability and purpose.
- Is this work individualistic? Qualities of spontaneous immediacy and substance should be evident.

2. *Choose music appropriate for your type of ensemble.* Several factors must be considered when you are matching repertoire with an ensemble.

- Size of the group. Madrigals are not intended for 200-voice choruses.
- Sectional balance. Weak on tenors in your mixed choir? Consider SAB music.
- Maturity of the voices. Heavy Romantic period works may overtax young singers.
- Soloists. Keep your best soloists busy.

3. *Choose reliable editions.* Be on the lookout for the following potential weaknesses in printed music:

- Improper or clumsy editing of composers' original markings and notations
- Poor text translations
- Weak transcriptions of solo or instrumental works

PROGRAM CONSTRUCTION

Selections chosen around a prearranged theme, concept, or overall scheme will result in a better "package" presentation. The old expression "the sum is greater than the parts" only holds true for programs which have been successfully organized.

Constructing a program obviously requires common sense. One should generally avoid placing an extremely demanding work at the beginning of a concert. Sandwiching short secular selections between serious sacred compositions of similar length is likewise to be avoided.

Formats

The following formats, used separately and in various combinations, have proven to be successful:

1. *Chronological.* A popular approach to programming. An example is:

- J. S. Bach, church cantata
- W. A. Mozart, motets
- Brahms, folk songs
- Romberg, operetta medley

2. *Thematic.* All or part of a program can be devoted to a central figure or idea. Some possibilities are:

- Compositions by the same composer. This approach allows for an in-depth acquaintance with one composer's output.
- Works from the same genre. I once performed a successful "Festival of Magnificats."
- Choral cycles. These include not only groups of songs by one composer but also cycles made up from isolated compositions. How about performing "Songs of Nature"?

3. *High interest/serious/light.* Takes into account the audience's mood and level of concentration.

- The opening group of selections could be festive.
- The middle choices could be more subdued and perhaps mood conscious.
- The concluding section could be devoted to folk songs or perhaps a Broadway medley.

4. *Contrast within unity.* Selections by vocal soloists and smaller groups can be interspersed with performances by the entire ensemble.

- Unity will be preserved by incorporating any of the other suggested formats.
- Variety can be achieved by juxtaposing pieces with contrasting moods.

5. *Featured work.* Quite often a lengthy major composition is selected first. If time allows, other shorter works can be chosen to fit around the primary choice.

- The major work can be "framed" by two selections serving as prelude and postlude.

- A serious major work can be followed, after intermission, by a group of lighter selections.

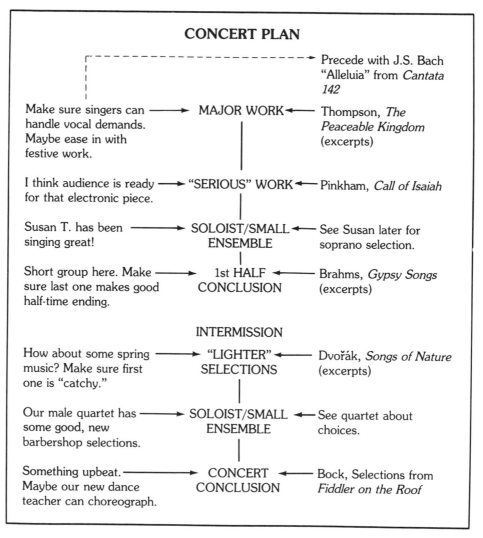

CONCERT PLAN

		Precede with J.S. Bach "Alleluia" from *Cantata 142*
Make sure singers can handle vocal demands. Maybe ease in with festive work.	→ MAJOR WORK ←	Thompson, *The Peaceable Kingdom* (excerpts)
I think audience is ready for that electronic piece.	→ "SERIOUS" WORK ←	Pinkham, *Call of Isaiah*
Susan T. has been singing great!	→ SOLOIST/SMALL ENSEMBLE ←	See Susan later for soprano selection.
Short group here. Make sure last one makes good half-time ending.	→ 1st HALF CONCLUSION ←	Brahms, *Gypsy Songs* (excerpts)
	INTERMISSION	
How about some spring music? Make sure first one is "catchy."	→ "LIGHTER" SELECTIONS ←	Dvořák, *Songs of Nature* (excerpts)
Our male quartet has some good, new barbershop selections.	→ SOLOIST/SMALL ENSEMBLE ←	See quartet about choices.
Something upbeat. Maybe our new dance teacher can choreograph.	→ CONCERT CONCLUSION ←	Bock, Selections from *Fiddler on the Roof*

Figure 2–3

An Approach to Planning

Quite often, when I construct a general type of concert program not geared to a specific theme, I rely on a "structural thought process" which has proven effective. Figure 2–3 presents my approach to planning a spring concert for a mixed choral ensemble based on my knowledge of the singers, the audience, and repertoire possibilities. Note how my thoughts and ideas are used to "flesh out" the structure.

CHAPTER 3

MANAGING THE PROGRAM

The following comment was recently made by a school administrator:

> My biggest headache is dealing with "artsy-craftsy" musicians. They're always disrupting the school schedule with last minute concerts and extra rehearsals. They overspend their budgets. They don't understand our procedures. Just last week, our vocal teacher tied up the Xerox machine for forty-five minutes making extra copies of music she forgot to order.

What kind of a reputation do you have as a businessperson? Are you prompt and reliable? Or, are you inefficient and impractical?

ESTABLISHING BUSINESS PROCEDURES

"Doing good business" means keeping on top of things. It also means knowing how to access information quickly so that you can make decisions and react to requests with minimal "down time."

Setting Up Shop

Whether you work out of a large "choral activities" office complete with secretaries and computers or you work out of your home as a "free-lance" conductor, you will need to establish an isolated "center of operations," then accumulate sufficient tools and resources to do your job. The following items are essential:

1. *Supplies.* When was the last time you ran down the hall to borrow someone's stapler? Make sure you have the essential nuts and bolts. Your list of items will range from paper clips to stationery with official letterhead. Some less obvious items you may also need, include:

- Colored pencils to mark your conductor's scores
- Stamps and pads to mark singers' music

- Cardboard for posters
- Personal bulletin board for messages and phone numbers

2. *Filing system.* A filing cabinet with folders is absolutely essential to survive. My present system includes the following categories:

- Music suppliers and catalogs
- Wardrobe suppliers and brochures
- Equipment suppliers and catalogs
- Inactive correspondence
- Active correspondence
- Old concert programs
- Musicians' names, addresses, and phone numbers
- Teaching aid supplies and catalogs
- Singers' audition/biographical forms
- Budget
- Potential concerts
- Tour and transportation agencies
- Records and reports

3. *Forms.* Almost every organization has its own "official" forms. Stocking up now will save time later. Examples include:

- Budget worksheets
- Student grade and data forms
- Award certificates
- Inventory checklists
- Annual report formats
- Attendance sheets

4. *Reference books.* Establish a nucleus of books which provide essential information for fast research. A good dictionary is a necessity. Music categories include:

- Conducting and rehearsing

- Vocal technique
- Diction
- Choral repertoire
- Choral history and literature
- General music history
- Stylistic interpretation
- Music theory, form and analysis
- Acoustics
- Terminology

Get with the Action!

Every organization has its own way of doing things. Make sure you understand procedures, then follow them as well as you possibly can. (See Situation 3–A.) This does not mean a faulty business practice should go unchallenged. But a good rule of thumb is to "go with the flow" until you have the chance to tactfully suggest a change.

Many problems encountered can be traced directly to *timeliness*. Perhaps it's better to "burn the midnight oil" if it's necessary to meet deadlines. Why run the risk of being labelled an "unreliable procrastinator"?

SITUATION 3–A

Larry O. was a part-time ensemble director at a large university. He needed music in a hurry, so he telephoned an order to a music publisher without getting requisition approval from the business office. When the bill arrived, the purchasing officer was unable to determine who ordered the music, why it was ordered, and which account was involved.

Based on personal experience and conversations with other choral directors, I have devised "Ten Commandments for Managing the Choral Program." (Figure 3–1.)

TEN COMMANDMENTS FOR MANAGING THE CHORAL PROGRAM

Thou shalt . . .

1. Attend to all business dealings promptly and reliably.
2. Allow for inevitable delays in the procurement of music, supplies, and equipment.
3. Clearly establish responsibilities and guidelines for those who work for you.
4. Understand and abide by established administrative practices and procedures.
5. Systematically account for and maintain music, wardrobe, and equipment.
6. Correspond with neatly typed or handwritten letters, addressed properly, on appropriate stationery.
7. Submit requests and reports in a timely manner, using correct forms and following prescribed formats.
8. Adopt a pleasing telephone manner, taking care to properly acknowledge and respond to others.
9. Make informed choices of merchandise to ensure that the product is of enduring value.
10. Never run out of music or supplies.

Figure 3–1

Management is an Ongoing Process

Good choral directors are more than good musicians. They are also good business administrators. As managers, they are continually involved in an ongoing process of planning, organizing, executing, and evaluating. Here are some of the things choral directors find themselves doing:

- Purchasing
- Providing
- Maintaining
- Communicating
- Publicizing
- Monitoring

Figure 3–2 presents a typical scenario for managing the choral program on an annual basis.

SCENARIO FOR MANAGING THE CHORAL PROGRAM

Pre-season: Order music, recordings, supplies, wardrobe, and teaching aids

Plan with officers and accompanists

Line up concerts

Communicate with new and returning singers

Prepare for auditions

Pre-rehearsals: Prepare music for dissemination

Tune piano

Ready the rehearsal room

Duplicate handouts for dissemination

Continual: Take attendance

Pay bills and maintain budget

Maintain equipment and supplies

Meet with key personnel

Raise money

Submit required reports

Pre-concerts: Disseminate wardrobe

Publicize

Print concert programs

Provide transportation

Post-season: Collect and store music and wardrobe

Assign grades

Submit budget requests for next year

Figure 3–2

BUILDING PUBLIC RELATIONS

Few choral ensembles can exist without publicity. Even the church choir, blessed with a weekly captive audience, occasionally needs to inform others about its special Sunday afternoon concert or announce a drive for new members.

Some school systems and colleges have publicity or community relations offices; others do not. But one thing is certain: *you* are ultimately responsible for your choral program's public relations. An enterprising publicity office may expedite matters by opening up avenues of communication and even taking pictures. It is up to you, however, to generate news and reach out to your public.

Organizing for Public Relations

Most people think of newspapers or radio and television when the word "publicity" is mentioned. Actually, *any* avenue which gives your group exposure, including word-of-mouth or even a concert, is a form of publicity. (See Situation 3–B.) Some other channels of communication available are:

- Telephone
- Brochures
- Mailed programs
- Posters
- Letters
- Magazines
- Recordings made by the ensemble

SITUATION 3–B

Paul M. wanted to advertise his summer concert to be held near Atlantic City, New Jersey. He hired an airplane advertiser to tow a banner along nearby beaches. The concert was packed!

The Ingredients of Good Publicity

Many choral directors appreciate the value of publicity but are not effective in this area of responsibility. Usually, this is because they do not understand the principles behind good publicity.

1. *Message.* What are the important facts we want to communicate? Will this information help us to reach our goals?
2. *Medium.* Which channels of communication will work best for each message? How can we exploit these avenues for better publicity?

3. *Newsworthiness.* Can we tailor our messages to make them acceptable for the media? What approaches will we employ to make our facts appealing and interesting?

4. *Clarity.* How clearly do we present information? Can we "pack in" more factual data with less verbiage?

5. *Timing.* When is the most advantageous time to release our message? Do we allow for procedural lags?

Developing a Nose for News

Newspapers are always looking for the following types of news:

1. *Spot news* consists of current information of immediate interest to readers. This week's concert or recently elected officers are good examples.

2. *Feature news* is based on human interest stories. Often this information has no immediacy and can be sent for release at any time. The lifestyle of the twins selected to be your joint accompanists would make feature news.

3. *Photo news* usually takes the form of a picture supported by a caption or brief article. I prefer to provide publicity photographs for this purpose.

Preparing the Press Release

The press release is the proper instrument for getting information to newspapers, magazines, as well as radio and television stations.

1. *Mechanics.* The release should be typed, using double or triple spacing. Use one side of an 8½ by 11 inch piece of plain white paper. Your name, the organization, address, and telephone number should be placed in the upper left-hand corner. In the upper right-hand corner, give the date and indicate whether the story should receive immediate or delayed release. If you make a typing error, do not erase or attempt to type over it. Black it out or "XXXX" over it with the typewriter. Clarity is important; neatness is immaterial. Check to see that all dates and times are correct and names accurately spelled. If a name, word, or title has an unusual spelling, type the letters "CQ" in parentheses after it to verify that the spelling is correct.

2. *Content.* Anyone can write a proper press release if the necessary ingredients of who, what, where, when, why, and how are included. Avoid

unnecessary verbiage and refrain from editorializing, unless you are requested
to do so by the editor. This includes describing a composition as "beautiful"
or designating someone as "talented." It is permissible, however, to quote the
subjective statements of a critic or writer.

Printed Materials

Most choral directors limit their printing requirements to concert
programs. Quite often, however, a professionally prepared poster or advertise-
ment will achieve greater results than a handmade notice or simple press
release.

Choosing a Logo

The use of a distinctive symbol or emblem is a great marketing tool. It is
remarkable how well small children can remember the names of professional
football teams simply by catching a glimpse of helmet logos. Figure 3–3
presents an example of a multi-purpose poster I use for one of my choral
ensembles. Note the use of a logo and an open fill-in space for providing
additional information. I have several hundred of these posters made at the
beginning of the school year at a reduced cost-per-item. They are 12 by 18
inches and are printed with bright red ink.

Figure 3–3

THE PRINTED PROGRAM

The printed program is intended to attractively provide essential information about your concert's repertoire and its participants. Just how much

information is necessary will depend on the formality of the concert. A short midday presentation would probably require only a brief listing of works to be performed, and the director might verbally announce supplementary information such as the names of soloists. On the other hand, a formal concert would require a full printed program, which might include all of the following information:

1. *Program cover or heading.* (See Figure 3–4.) As with good newspaper reporting, several basic questions must be immediately answered for the program reader.

- Who? What performing group is involved? If several ensembles will perform, they may be listed separately or given a collective name such as "The Edison High School Choral Groups." The names of the director, accompanists, and soloists may also be listed here or within the context of the program repertoire.
- What? Describe the type of concert, whether it is simply "A Choral Concert" or a more specific type such as "The Third Annual Christmas Choral Pageant."
- Where? Even though the audience obviously knows where it is, the concert location should be provided. Programs are often filed for reference or passed on to others, and this information becomes necessary.
- When? Give the date, including the year, and the time of the concert.

2. *The repertoire to be performed.* (Figure 3–5.) Usually prefaced by the heading "Program," this part of your printed program must be carefully laid out so that your audience does not get lost. Care must be taken to set off groups of selections from one another by using double spacing. The names of ensembles should be printed in boldface type or capital letters. Soloists' names must be placed close to the title of the work in which the soloists will perform. Some further suggestions regarding program entries are:

- When listing composers' names, be specific. Remember, two members of the illustrious Bach family composed Magnificats. Be sure that you include first initials when you are dealing with composers with identical last names. Better yet, print full names and avoid such potential problems.
- List the complete title of program entries. "Kyrie Eleison" by Schubert does not give the listener sufficient information since we

THE
MOUNT UNION COLLEGE
CONCERT CHOIR
Dr. Lewis Gordon, Director

presents a
CONCERT OF TWENTIETH CENTURY
CHORAL MUSIC

composed by
COLLEGE MUSIC SOCIETY COMPOSERS

and featuring works by
OTTO LUENING

October 18, 1981
10:30 A.M.

College Music Society
Joint Meeting
with the
National Guild
of
Community Schools of the Arts
Cincinnati, Ohio

October 11, 1981
3:00 P.M.
First United Methodist Church
Akron, Ohio

November 4, 1981
8:30 P.M.
Mount Union College
Alliance, Ohio

Figure 3–4

PROGRAM

CONCERT CHOIR

Come Ye Sons of Art .... *Henry Purcell*

    1. Chorus - Come Ye Sons of Art
    2. Duet - Sound the Trumpet
    3. Chorus - The Honour of a Jubilee
    4. Duet - These are the Sacred Charms
    5. Chorus - See Nature, Rejoicing
              Melinda Miller, *Soprano Soloist*
         Victoria Strand, *Mezzo-Soprano Soloist*

Stabat Mater (First Movement) ..... *Giovanni Battista Pergolesi*

CHAMBER SINGERS

Vere Languores Nostros .... *Antonio Lotti*

Three English Madrigals

    1. While Joyful Springtime Lasteth .... *Henry Youll*
    2. Go, Wailing Accents .... *John Ward*
    3. How Merrily We Live .... *Michael East*

CONCERT CHOIR

Jubilate Deo Omnis Terra .... *Flor Peeters*

TRIO

The Nightingale .... *Thomas Bateson*

Fly Not So Fast .... *John Ward*

O Welcome Dear and Lovely May .... *Franz Schubert*
    Members: Mary Davenport, Nancy Teich, Sylvia Wood

CONCERT CHOIR

Three Hebrew Psalms .... *Michael Braz*

    1. Hiney Ma Tov
    2. Mi Chomocho
    3. Adonoy Yimloch

Three Hungarian Folk Songs .... *Bela Bartok*

    1. In the Village
    2. See the Roses
    3. Boatman! Boatman!

Figure 3–5

know that the composer wrote Kyries for six different Latin Masses. If the selection is taken from a larger work, let people know.

- Differentiate between composers and arrangers. *Shenandoah* was not composed by Gregg Smith; it was arranged by him (as well as others). Use the abbreviation "Arr." before arrangers' names.

3. *Supplementary information.* The following items should be considered for each printed program:

- *Translations.* It is usually helpful to provide listeners with translations of foreign texts performed in the concert. Very short translations can be included within the program of repertoire. More lengthy translations should be placed on another page of the printed program or distributed separately.

- *Program notes.* These may include background information about musical selections or biographical data on individual performers. Newsworthy items about the ensemble or upcoming auditions are also worth listing.

- *Participating musicians.* Keep in mind that concerts are performed by people who appreciate seeing their names on a program, especially if the event has personal significance for them. The concertgoer may not know 95 percent of the performers, but you can be sure that he or she will be looking on the printed program for familiar names.

- *Sponsors.* Individuals or businesses who have contributed financially toward the choral organization deserve mention in your program.

- *Acknowledgments.* Quite often others are partly responsible for your concert's success. These individuals may range from the orchestra director who helped to prepare the instrumental accompaniment to students who sold tickets for the presentation. While a handshake or a letter of appreciation is always welcomed, the best way to show your appreciation is by noting these people and their contributions in your printed program.

Program Appeal

The printed program does far more than provide essential information; it also *conditions* the audience for the concert. The expectant mood created within the listener often depends on the printed program's appearance as well as its content. For example, if you attended a formal evening concert, how would your attitude be affected by a poorly spaced, half-faded, slightly angled program duplicated on a "ditto" machine?

Needless to say, printed programs can be expensive for a small ensemble operating on a shoestring budget. Sometimes, however, imagination and attention to detail can offset financial limitations. Consider the following:

1. *Physical layout.* The number of pages in a program is, for the most part, controlled by the amount of information to be printed. The size and design of those pages, however, is open to far more ingenious ideas than the standard rectangular format.

- Experiment with unusually wide or long pages. Printers can reduce letter size to comfortably fit an entire program of repertoire on a 6 by 12 inch sheet of paper.
- Consider programs with rounded corners or scalloped edges.
- Have programs folded accordion style into several pages.

2. *Color and texture.* A visit to the printer's shop will reward you with a surprising discovery of what is available for printed programs.

- Consider the wide latitude of light colored and textured paper now available.
- Choose different colors for printing. Dark red ink on light beige paper is very effective.
- Have the program run off on several different pastel colored packs of paper. Then, shuffle these various colored programs before distributing them to the audience. This approach is especially effective for festivals and lighter concerts.

3. *Print.* Most programs are too conservative in their use of print to set off titles, names of ensembles, and so on.

- Request printers to use lettering of various heights and thicknesses.
- Choose print which matches the type of program you will be presenting. Old English lettering goes well with Renaissance programs; sleek print looks good for contemporary programs.

Supervising the Printing of the Program

Many choral concerts have been blemished by printed programs which omitted information or contained misspelled names. I once approved for printing a beautiful program which failed to mention the name of the performing group! Care must be especially taken when you are dealing with peoples' names. Is your accompanist's first name Marianne, Maryanne, or Mary Ann?

Directors sometimes falsely assume that scribbling out a program for the secretary to type is sufficient. The only way to ensure the printed program's success is through follow-up action. Even when an officer or choral secretary has been given responsibility for this project, you are accountable for the finished product. The following steps will help to guarantee the program's success:

- Start by typing a rough draft to determine spacing and overall layout.

- Type a final draft and proofread it before sending it to the printer.

- Request galley proofs from the printer and proofread these before approving the actual printing.

Proofreaders sometimes fall into the trap of reading programs for content rather than accuracy. For this reason it is a good idea to have a second proofreader.

When you are ordering programs, be sure that you request enough for an unexpected bumper crop of listeners. People will share if they have to, but running out of programs is like inviting guests for dinner and not having enough food. Finally, provide typists and printers with sufficient time to meet your concert deadlines comfortably. When you are using professional printers, plan to have weekend concert programs delivered the Thursday before the presentation. This allows an extra day for delivery vehicle breakdown, unexpected snowstorms, and the like.

MUSIC, WARDROBE, AND EQUIPMENT

Can you complete all of the following tasks in ten minutes or less?

- Order five more scores of Handel's *Messiah*.

- Determine who checked out copy 23 of last year's Easter cantata.

- Find out how blazer 17 became stained.

- Make arrangements to have your school tape recorder serviced under warranty.

Did you pass the test? If not, you probably need to establish more consistent procedures for purchasing, storing, and maintaining choral-related items.

Music Purchasing and Handling

I have directed choral ensembles in various parts of the country. Through trial and error, I have discovered the necessity of locating reliable music dealers who are compatible with my present choral situation. When choosing your dealer, consider the following criteria:

- Is service efficient and reliable?
- Can the dealer relate to your needs, style choices, and make recommendations?
- Does the dealer push only "in house" stock, or can you expect a determined effort to locate esoteric or foreign publications?
- Will the dealer provide free preview (perusal) service or complimentary copies?
- Is a discount offered for bulk orders?

Music dealers sometimes change their merchandising preferences. I recently stopped purchases from a large national distributor because it began specializing in light contemporary music at the expense of more standard fare. It's also good to have an account with more than one dealer. I know a choral director who purchases all of her women's repertoire from a separate dealer because the order clerk is a treble choir "expert."

Ordering Music

Before buying music, try to obtain as much information as you can about a particular work. If you order *O Sing Unto the Lord* by Hassler, an unsuspecting clerk may conclude that no editions exist. However, an enterprising dealer might be able to provide you with at least three editions, listed under the work's original title, *Cantate Domino*.

Send away for publishers' and dealers' catalogs. Better yet, build your own library of single copies of music. When ordering, try to provide the following information:

- Composer (and/or arranger)
- Title
- Voicing
- Publisher
- Octavo number

- Price
- Number of copies

As a rule of thumb, order 5 percent more copies than you need. This will allow for unexpected new ensemble members and for loss of copies. Your order usually will be sent by fourth class mail. If you need the music in a hurry, specify first class, parcel post, or special carrier.

Disseminating and Accounting for Music

When new music arrives from a publisher or distributor, it should be immediately numbered and stamped with the choral organization's name. This is the only way to control the dissemination of music. Each singer is assigned a folder (preferably with storage pockets) labelled by name and number, and a record of this is kept. When the new music is ready for distribution, it can be spread out on a table in numerical order. This saves time by allowing the member to locate his or her numbered copy before the rehearsal begins. Make sure all singers are aware of your procedures and advise them of the following suggested regulations:

- Members are responsible for loss or damage of music and folder.
- Avoid exposure to inclement weather.
- Use pencil only.

Occasionally directors from other organizations want to borrow music, or singers in your group would like to review selections not included in their current repertoire. For these purposes an index card file of music checked out to special individuals must be maintained. Information should include:

- Date music was checked out
- Title of music
- Number of copies
- Intended due date
- Signature of person checking out music

When you are storing the organization's music, alphabetical filing by composer or title rather than seasonal or functional classification works best. For example, Magnificats are usually considered to be Christmas music, but they may be performed at other times of the year. In smaller choral libraries simply placing octavo music alphabetically and doing the same with larger works will enable you to choose possible selections by scanning. Larger libraries, however, require a separate card index system. As new music is added to the organization's collection, the following information should be logged in:

- Composer's name
- Title of work
- Publisher
- Choral scoring
- Number of copies
- Performance time
- Filed location

Storing Music

Printed music should be protected from dust and mishandling yet be readily accessible when needed. Vertical folders in file cabinets work adequately for short octavo works. Expandable manila filing folders are also popular. I use filing boxes, available in various widths and depths from music merchandisers. These can be stored vertically on shelves. Oversized works and large scores are best stacked flat inside cabinets with side-entry doors.

In many organizations the singers' personal folders and music are stored between rehearsals. In such situations storage cabinets should be provided. Each bin should then be assigned by name or number. Footlockers containing vertical panels spaced two or three inches apart are ideal for storing music on concert tours.

Wardrobe

Building or replacing a complete wardrobe for a sizeable choral ensemble is expensive. Furthermore, the chosen product will be scrutinized by hundreds of concert attenders. Figure 3–6 presents various types of wearing apparel with advantages and disadvantages.

Commercial robes are hard to beat for price as well as quality. One alternative is to purchase blazers for men, then have matching vests made for the women. Used tuxedos or outdated styles are sometimes available at reduced cost from local formal shops. (See Situation 3–C.)

WEARING APPAREL

Type	Advantages	Disadvantages
Dresses and Suits	No organizational outlay of money	Lack of uniformity
Robes	Uniform appearance Flexibility in fitting Moderate cost Easy to don	Sacred connotation
Blazers	Snappy looking for men Good for secular ensembles	Restrictive for women Need uniformity in slacks and skirts
Tuxedos	Very distinctive	Difficult to size Expensive
Formal gowns	Elegant	Difficult to keep clean and re-use

Figure 3–6

SITUATION 3–C

Wayne C. came across fifty tuxedos in the neighborhood formal shop. Grooms wouldn't rent them because they were powder blue. He purchased them for twenty-five dollars each, then sold them to his male chorus. Townsfolk claim they have the flashiest glee club in the state.

Women's skirts and dresses can be made at considerable savings, especially if the material is purchased wholesale directly from factory outlets. Choose a basic color that can be easily matched should later purchases be required. If a dressmaker is used, make sure you buy extras.

Assigning and Storing Wardrobe

Each wardrobe item must be identified by a permanently affixed number. These may be sewn in or marked with an indelible pen. A record of assignment must be accurately maintained, and singers must be clearly informed of their responsibility to return items punctually and in good repair. Closets work best for storage because they minimize dust. Metal wardrobe cabinets are also available at most business equipment stores. Garments should not hang unprotected in a large room. Use dust covers or storage bags in these instances.

Equipment

Would you purchase the first new car you saw without comparing it for quality and price with others? I have seen choral musicians take this approach when buying equipment—even pianos—for their program. Use the following procedure when selecting equipment and you will come out a "satisfied customer":

- Research the item to determine which type or model will best serve your needs.
- Gather brochures and specifications from manufacturers for comparison.
- Determine warranty backing and servicing quality where applicable.
- Shop for lowest cost without sacrificing quality or service.

Risers

Wider widths will allow for chairs and can be used for everyday rehearsals as well as for nearby concerts. Narrower, lightweight risers are best for performance only but can be carried on tours. Options include carpeting, casters for rolling, and railings. Reflectors (shells) are ideal for heavily curtained stages, expansive concert halls, and outdoor situations.

Video and Sound Recording Equipment

Local dealers offer a variety of models, often on sale. A large video screen (monitor) will allow you to show educational video tapes and recordings to your entire ensemble. Choose quality microphones for distortion-free sound recording.

Maintenance

Upkeep of choral organization property is another practical necessity. Unfortunately, it is a chore sometimes overlooked until a serious problem arises. Ideally, maintenance and housekeeping should be fully entrusted to custodial staff and hired technicians. More often, however, it requires your close attention. The piano that was "supposed to have been tuned" could turn a concert into a real disaster. Sometimes incidental duties, such as replacing a burned-out music stand lamp, are best handled by the director. The following areas of concern should be periodically checked and action taken as necessary:

1. *Keyboard instruments.* Besides maintaining proper intonation, check for physical abuse, cleanliness, and foreign objects inside.
2. *Wardrobe.* Look for physical wear (especially frayed cuffs), spots, stains around the collar, and excessive wrinkles.
3. *Music folders.* Repair tears with invisible mending tape. Replace unusable copies.
4. *High fidelity equipment.* Be on the lookout for inoperative speakers, unusual hums, and faulty mechanical operation.
5. *Lights and lamps.* Check for burned out bulbs, frayed wires, and loose fixtures.

RAISING MONEY

Some choral organizations are financially well off; others are not so fortunate. There are three basic reasons why most singing groups should consider raising money for themselves.

1. *To survive.* Many vocal ensembles exist independently from any sponsoring organization. For them, finding enough money to cover operating costs is a "do or die" issue.

2. *To augment the budget.* Sometimes choirs have the money to survive but want to enhance the quality of their program by bringing in additional revenue. Maybe this extra money can be used to hire instrumentalists. Another excellent reason would be to establish a scholarship fund or donate the profits to a worthy cause.

3. *To meet the costs of special projects.* Sooner or later, unusual expenses create a sudden demand for extra money. Good examples would be replacing

a worn-out wardrobe or purchasing a new piano. Choir tours and special invitations to perform in distant places create similar demands.

Sources

Several potential avenues of financial support are available. But, before pursuing these courses of action, the director of a church or school choir should be certain that he has already received maximum funding for his group. For example, I proposed a special concert for the bicentennial celebration and received additional money to cover costs involved. Sometimes an extra push can spring loose extra financial support.

Sources for additional money depend on the nature of the organization. A church choir cannot depend on alumni for support, and elementary school choruses do not usually qualify for foundation grants. Here is a list of primary sources.

1. *The members themselves.* Dues are an effective means for covering minimal costs or augmenting budgets. The annual banquet is a typical expenditure for this type of income. Watch out, however, that a sudden levy or increase in fees does not result in a loss of membership.

2. *Parents and friends.* Younger performers cannot pay for such expenses as a foreign choir tour, but their parents may support the idea if it seems promising. In adult ensembles friends of members are often sympathetic to the choral group's goals and frequently attend its concerts. Direct correspondence soliciting financial support can reap monetary rewards.

3. *Alumni.* Memories of the "good old days" are usually filled with sights, *sounds*, and events. For many graduates the alma mater choir or glee club still has symbolic significance. If you work closely with alumni officers, a solid avenue of financial support can be established. Don't overlook the possibility of borrowing money from your alumni association. One school choral group which I directed received a three-year loan to purchase a new wardrobe. The money was repaid (interest free) in annual installments by the student activities fund.

4. *Community.* Local businesses can be a tremendous source of funds, especially if their owners know that they will receive publicity for support. Some corporations encourage their branches and divisions to spend money locally each year to further public relations. —What better way than to aid your choral group!

Quality ensembles sometimes draw a following of individuals who would be more than willing to make a contribution if asked. Make an attempt to draw the community closer to the organization's values and goals by actively soliciting support.

5. *Grants.* Public and private foundations at the local, state, and national levels are often on the lookout for enterprising cultural activities worthy of their support. Usually, however, you have to find *them* and convince them of your particular choral program's value. The following hints are offered:

- Sell the program's advantages over other groups. ("My ensemble performs frequently for charitable causes.")
- Pinpoint its uniqueness. ("This vocal group specializes in early period music.")
- Provide proof of its success. ("The *Townsville Times* wrote the following rave review about our last choral performance . . .")

Methods

Procedures for raising money may be relatively conventional like charging admission to a concert and soliciting advertisements for a printed program; or they might be highly imaginative. Have you ever thought of selling fire extinguishers during Fire Prevention Week? Effective methods for funding the organization are as diversified as creativity itself.

When you are beginning a financial drive, it is a good idea to elect or appoint a campaign chairman so that all aspects of the plan will be properly administered and coordinated. If items are to be sold, these can be purchased directly from a wholesaler. Several merchandising businesses offer special plans for organizations interested in raising money for themselves. Here are just a few examples of profit-making projects:

- Make a recording of your group and sell records for profit (great for alumni support!).
- Hold benefit concerts, with the proceeds going to a choir tour, for a charity organization, and so on. Sell tickets or take up a collection.
- Sell candy, handmade jewelry, or baked goods.
- Hold an auction.
- Show movies and charge admission.
- Hold a lottery.
- Conduct a "sing in." The audience pays admission to participate in the performance of a well-known choral work.
- Wash cars, serve spaghetti dinners, paint houses.

OFFICERS—FIGUREHEADS OR CRUCIAL WORKERS?

The decision whether or not to have choral group officers often rests with the director. Some organizations, however, have well-established committees charged with the power of hiring and firing conductors. The choral leader's role will therefore depend on the nature of each situation.

- With education ensembles, the director should serve as an adviser and encourage student officers to make responsible decisions.
- With adult choral groups, the director should choose the role of trouble-shooter by making recommendations for smoother, more efficient operation.

Are Officers Really Necessary?

Small church choirs seldom need officers because of the relatively straightforward operation of the music program. Sometimes a single member is given the responsibility of looking after the wardrobe. Otherwise the director handles all duties as part of the job. Professional and university choral groups often hire a business manager or secretary.

Regardless of who makes the decision to choose officers, one thing is certain: they must have a purpose. This means that responsibilities must be split between the director and the officers. In some cases conductors allow officers to participate in repertoire selection; in other instances directors prefer to reserve certain nonmusical decisions for themselves. For example, I line up concert appearances and then turn the responsibility of working out the details to my officers. A very practical solution is as follows:

- The director makes all musical decisions.
- The officers carry out supportive and supplemental duties.

Officers' Individual Responsibilities

Officers' responsibilities will vary among organizations and should be tailored to fit each situation. A small group might appoint a music librarian who also handles correspondence. Figure 3–7 presents a full complement of officers and their suggested areas of responsibility for a large choral organization.

```
┌─────────────────────────────────────────────────────────────┐
│                  OFFICERS' RESPONSIBILITIES                   │
│                                                               │
│  President . . . . . . . . . . . . . . . . . . . overall leadership and coordination │
│  Vice President . . . . . . . . . . . . . . . publicity, transportation, and │
│                                              supplies         │
│  Secretary . . . . . . . . . . . . . . . . . . attendance, correspondence, and │
│                                              communication with members │
│  Treasurer . . . . . . . . . . . . . . . . . financial affairs │
│  Librarian . . . . . . . . . . . . . . . . . music and wardrobe │
└─────────────────────────────────────────────────────────────┘
```

Figure 3–7

Guidelines for Effectual Operation

Sometimes relationships and responsibilities between the director and the officers are allowed to deteriorate. I have known conductors who gradually assumed more and more responsibility because of undedicated officers. Some suggestions for maintaining a smooth administrative liaison with your officers include:

- Keep them informed of all decisions you have made.

- Use the chain of command. For example, do not make a decision with the treasurer without including the president in your plans.

- Allow your officers to make proper decisions and support their choices.

- Give them credit whenever it is due.

- If your officers need guidance, provide them with procedural checklists and outlines.

CHAPTER 4

ESTABLISHING RUDIMENTS OF CONDUCTING

One of the most important attributes of a successful choral director is the desire to master and improve conducting skills.

BASIC CONDUCTING—WHAT IT MUST ACCOMPLISH

The primary purpose of conducting is to guide an ensemble through the performance of a musical composition. The methods used to achieve this goal have varied throughout the history of musical performance. For example, Jean Baptiste Lully, the notable French Baroque composer-conductor, utilized a long wooden staff to beat time during orchestral performances. Unfortunately, he stomped his foot and died of terminal infection.

Gesticulation

Today's conductors have become far more sophisticated at guiding ensembles by use of functional sign language which we call gesticulation. When developed and utilized to its fullest, gesticulation will fulfill the following functions:

1. *It will account for time and place within music.* This is achieved by the use of conducting patterns indicating movement through measures.
2. *It will prepare performers for musical action.* Ensemble members are forewarned of attacks and entries by conducting cues.
3. *It will coordinate and regulate the technical aspects of performance.* Dynamics, articulation, and changes in tempo are deliniated by controlled arm and hand movement.

The Baton

The controversy of whether or not to use a baton while conducting has persisted for many years. Most arguments on both sides can be narrowed down to the following views:

- The baton offers more clarity and precision than the hand.
- The hand offers more expressive possibilities than the baton.

One way to reach a solution is by asking the musicians themselves which method they prefer. Based on personal experience and discussions with other conductors and ensemble performers, I have found a clear indication that singers usually feel more comfortable with the free hand and instrumentalists prefer the baton unless they are performing in a small chamber group.

I personally take the position that a choral director should become adept at conducting both with and without the baton. By developing the flexibility to conduct either way, you can choose the method which will best fit the situation. This decision should be based on the following two considerations:

1. The chosen method should be determined by the proportion and importance of vocal and instrumental forces required in a particular work. For example, Beethoven's "Choral Symphony" would best be conducted with a baton, whereas J. S. Bach's motets, performed with instrumental doubling, might prosper better under the guidance of a free hand.

2. You could elect to employ *both* methods within the same work. This is especially appropriate where *a cappella* movements are sandwiched between instrumentally accompanied sections. Ralph Vaughan Williams' *Hodie* is an example of such construction.

The discussions of right-hand activity as well as the patterns contained in this chapter are oriented toward conducting without a baton.

Conducting Patterns

Some choral directors contend that there is little need for adhering to fundamental conducting patterns. They argue that these patterns are too mechanistic for choral performance, that they interfere with interpretive gesturing. Fortunately, it is possible for the choral director to "have his cake and eat it too." Simply put, a conducting pattern which has been developed into a habitual response can be modified to accommodate musical expression without losing directional integrity. Furthermore, if singers are to develop into musicians, they will need to know where the beat lies. According to Wilhelm Ehmann, noted German conductor and educator,

> There still is no other device in choral work which offers the possibility of the same security, precision, thoroughness and economy of energy as the mastery of a sound time-beating technique.[1]

---

[1] Wilhelm Ehmann, *Choral Directing*, Trans. George D. Wiebe (Minneapolis: Augsburg Publishing House, 1968), p. 114.

Conducting patterns should be mastered to the extent that they will be technically secure and precise under a variety of "battlefield" conditions. Preoccupation with images of printed conducting diagrams must give way to *habitual* responses which are cued by the music itself. (See Situation 4–A.)

SITUATION 4–A

George L. was a good choral conductor with an unusual habit. When attending others' concerts, he would become totally engrossed in the music and begin to conduct, first with his fingers, then later with his hand. Once I sat next to him and noticed he always chose the correct pattern!

In many instances, there is more than one established method for executing conducting patterns, cutoffs, etc. My intention is to provide you with *one* basic approach founded on accepted principles of conducting.

PHYSICAL READINESS FOR CONDUCTING

Before you begin to conduct, you must assume correct posture. This initial step is important for you as well as for your singers.

- It places you in an optimal position to conduct with maximum effectiveness.
- It alerts the singers that you are ready to begin.
- It sets an example for them to also assume proper posture for singing.

The Components of Good Posture

1. *Feet.* They should be approximately shoulder width apart and even with each other. Your weight should be distributed slightly forward.
2. *Chest.* It should be comfortably high. This position can be established by raising your arms, fully extended, over your head, then *slowly* lowering them without allowing the chest to lower.
3. *Alignment.* The upper torso should be straight. Avoid a protruding chin and a protruding posterior. Your legs should be slightly bent, or they may also be straight but not rigid.

4. *Arms.* In preparation for conducting, the arms should be extended until the tips of the hands are between 12 and 16 inches from the body at chest level. The exact distance will be dependent on your height. Overextension will weaken your appearance and create a tendency to lean forward while conducting. Underextension will restrict your arm movement.

5. *Hands.* Their configuration will vary depending on the mood of the music and the type of articulation desired. For purposes of initial development, the fingers should be extended and touching yet be relaxed and slightly curved. The thumb should be allowed to separate slightly from the index finger.

Evaluating Your Readiness for Conducting

The best way to prepare yourself physically for conducting is to locate a wall mirror—preferably floor length—so that you may evaluate your posture and your facial expression. The mirror will also be helpful throughout your development as a conductor.

Exercise 1: Assume correct posture using The Components of Good Posture as a guide. Check your mirror image and make necessary spot corrections.

Exercise 2: Imagine that you are ready to conduct a musical composition. Assume correct posture and look at yourself in the mirror. Now convince yourself through facial expression that you are ready to actually begin. Does your intent show? Experiment by varying your facial expressions.

CONDUCTING BASIC PATTERNS

Before examining specific patterns, let's compare them for their similarities.

General Characteristics of Conducting Patterns

Although conducting patterns differ from each other in their configuration, they share several common characteristics.

1. *Patterns are traditionally conducted with the right hand.* The left hand is utilized for other activities such as cueing and shaping of musical phrases. This tradition often poses problems for left-handed persons.

However, once the patterns are mastered, left-handers usually develop left-hand gesticulation superior to that displayed by right-handers.

2. *The initiation of a conducting pattern requires a preparatory beat.* This extra stroke readies the performers for their attack. For singers, this is the moment of inhalation. To encourage adequate breathing, you should open your mouth and inhale while conducting the preparatory beat.

3. *The size of the conducting pattern is affected by ensemble size, tempo, and dynamics.* In small vocal groups singers have a close view of the conductor and can easily see a small pattern. Conversely, singers at a distance from the conductor in large ensembles require a larger pattern. Pattern size may also be affected by tempo. For example, it is difficult to conduct a large pattern at a fast tempo. Generally speaking, pattern size decreases as tempo increases. And finally, the size of a pattern is dependent on dynamics. The louder the music, the bigger the pattern and vice versa.

Establishing the Field of Beating

Patterns are conducted within a frame of operation called the field of beating. This field is deliniated by imaginary vertical and horizontal axes upon which the conducting patterns are superimposed. (See Figure 4–1.) Patterns are comprised of strokes, called beats, which move up, down, left, and right along the imaginary axes. In music the primary accents, which occur at the beginning of each measure, are indicated in conducting by a downbeat which moves along the vertical axis. The field of beating will vary in size, depending on the size of the pattern.

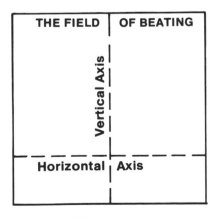

Figure 4–1

To establish your field of beating, you should perform the following exercise in front of a mirror:

"Conduct" an imaginary vertical axis by moving your right arm up and down. Do the same for a horizontal axis by moving the arm left and right. Make sure that the horizontal axis crosses the vertical axis approximately one-fourth of the way up from its lowest point. Note how far you moved along both axes. Now "draw" an imaginary box with your hand which touches the outermost points of the axes. This is your field of beating. Vary the field by "conducting" axes of varying lengths. Create rectangular as well as square boxes.

The One Pattern

The one pattern is typically used for fast-moving $\frac{3}{8}$ and $\frac{3}{4}$ meters. Conducting three beats per measure in these instances may be tiring for the conductor and confusing for the singers. Occasionally fast-moving works in $\frac{2}{4}$ are better conducted in one.

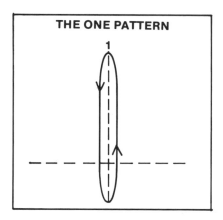

THE ONE PATTERN

Figure 4–2

Figure 4–2 shows that the one pattern is conducted as an eliptical circle which moves along the imaginary vertical axis. Movement is continuous. Avoid stopping at the top of the beat; rebound immediately at the bottom of the beat.

Conduct the following rhythm using the one pattern to establish one-to-the-measure control.

Allegro

NOTE: The preparatory beat is initiated by conducting one entire repetition of the pattern.

The Two Pattern

The two pattern is commonly used for music written in $\frac{2}{8}$, $\frac{2}{4}$, and cut time ($\mathcal{C}$), technically known as *alla breve*. It is also used for fast-moving $\frac{4}{8}$ and $\frac{6}{8}$ meters.

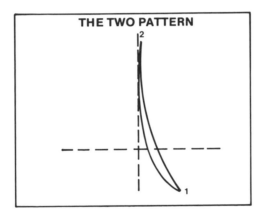

Figure 4–3

Figure 4–3 shows that the downbeat of the two pattern moves downward along the imaginary vertical axis. To avoid abruptness in the pattern, allow the arm to swing slightly to your right before reaching the pattern's termination. The upbeat moves upward, closely tracking the path made by the downbeat.

Conduct the following rhythms using the two pattern:

1.

NOTE: The preparatory beat is initiated by conducting the *upbeat* (the second beat).

2.

NOTE: The preparatory beat is initiated by conducting the *downbeat* (the first beat).

The Three Pattern

The three pattern is typically used for music written in $\frac{3}{8}$, $\frac{3}{4}$, and $\frac{3}{2}$ meter. It is also used for moderate to fast-moving $\frac{9}{8}$ meter.

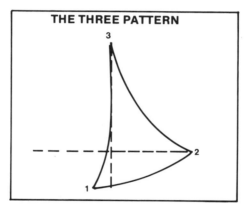

Figure 4–4

Figure 4–4 shows that the downbeat of the three pattern moves downward along the imaginary vertical axis. The second beat moves *to your right* and slightly upward until it reaches the horizontal axis. The third beat moves upward diagonally to the original position. To avoid abruptness in the pattern, allow the arm to curve slightly along the lines of direction as shown in the diagram.

Conduct the following rhythms using the three pattern:

1.

NOTE: The preparatory beat is initiated by conducting the *upbeat* (the third beat).

2.

NOTE: The preparatory beat is initiated by conducting the *downbeat* (the first beat).

3.

NOTE: The preparatory beat is initiated by conducting the *second beat*.

The Four Pattern

The four pattern is commonly used for music written in $\frac{4}{8}$, $\frac{4}{4}$, and $\frac{4}{2}$ meter. It is also used for moderate to fast-moving $\frac{12}{8}$ meter. Figure 4–5 shows that the downbeat of the four pattern moves downward along the imaginary vertical axis. The second beat moves *to your left* and slightly upward until it reaches the horizontal axis. The third beat moves to your right along the horizontal axis and *crossing* the vertical axis. The fourth beat moves upward diagonally to the original position. To avoid abruptness in the pattern, allow the arm to curve slightly along the lines of direction as shown in the diagram. Conduct exercises similar to those suggested for the previous conducting pattern.

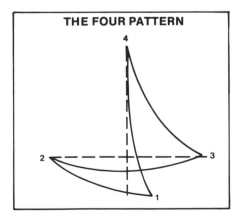

Figure 4–5

The Five Pattern

The five pattern is used for music written in $\frac{5}{8}$, $\frac{5}{4}$, and $\frac{5}{2}$ meter. Performers and conductors often have problems with this meter because of its unbalanced, asymmetrical structure. However, five-beat meters are becoming increasingly popular in contemporary choral music.

Two versions of the five pattern are traditionally employed, depending on the location of the secondary accent.

NOTE: Rhythmic patterns within five-beat measures tend to fall into groups of 2 + 3 (resulting in a secondary accent on the third beat) or 3 + 2 (resulting in a secondary accent on the fourth beat). In instances where groupings within measures do not occur, *either* conducting pattern may be used.

Figure 4–6 should be used when the secondary accent falls on the *third* beat. The downbeat moves downward along the imaginary vertical axis. The second beat moves to your left and slightly upward until it reaches the horizontal axis. The third beat moves to your right along the horizontal axis and *crossing* the vertical axis. The fourth beat moves upward and diagonally to the left. The fifth beat continues upward diagonally to the original position.

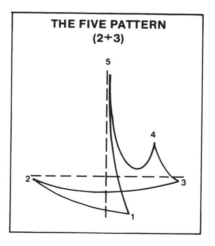

Figure 4–6

Figure 4–7 should be used when the secondary accent falls on the *fourth* beat. The downbeat moves downward along the imaginary vertical axis. The second beat moves slightly to your left and slightly upward. The third beat moves further to your left and slightly upward until it reaches the horizontal axis. The fourth beat moves to your right along the horizontal axis and *crossing* the vertical axis. The fifth beat moves upward diagonally to the original position. To avoid abruptness in the pattern, allow the arm to curve slightly along the lines of direction as shown in the diagram. Conduct exercises similar to those suggested for the three pattern.

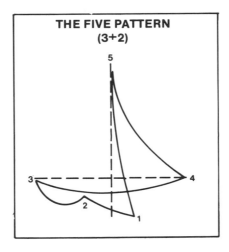

Figure 4–7

The Six Pattern

The six pattern is used for music written in $\frac{6}{8}$, $\frac{6}{4}$, and $\frac{6}{2}$ meter.

NOTE: Remember, the two pattern is employed for fast-moving $\frac{6}{8}$ meter.

The secondary accent naturally falls on the fourth beat. Figure 4–8 shows that the downbeat moves downward along the imaginary vertical axis. The second beat moves slightly to your left and slightly upward. The third beat moves further to your left and slightly upward until it reaches the horizontal axis. The fourth beat moves to your right along the horizontal axis and *crossing* the vertical axis. The fifth beat moves upward and diagonally to the left. The sixth beat continues upward and diagonally to the original position. To avoid abruptness in the pattern, allow the arm to curve slightly along the lines of direction as shown in the diagram.

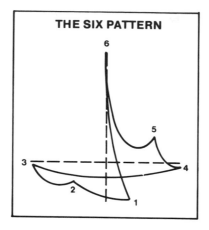

Figure 4–8

Conduct exercises similar to those suggested for the three pattern.

The Twelve Pattern

The twelve pattern is used for music written in $\frac{12}{8}$, $\frac{12}{4}$, and $\frac{12}{2}$ meter.

NOTE: Remember, the four pattern is employed for moderate and fast-moving $\frac{12}{8}$ meter.

The secondary accent naturally falls on the seventh beat. Figure 4–9 reveals what is essentially a four-beat type of pattern. Beats 1, 2, and 3 are

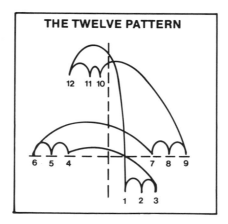

Figure 4–9

concentrated at the bottom of the imaginary vertical axis. The first beat is characterized by a direct, purposeful move. The second and third beats are achieved by gentle rebounding of the wrist and hand. Beats 4, 5, and 6 are concentrated at the left side of the imaginary horizontal axis. The fourth beat is characterized by a direct, purposeful move. The fifth and sixth beats are achieved by gentle rebounding. Beats 7, 8, and 9 are concentrated at the right side of the imaginary horizontal axis. The seventh beat is characterized by a direct, purposeful move. The eighth and ninth beats are achieved by gentle rebounding. Beats 10, 11, and 12 are concentrated at the top of the imaginary vertical axis. The tenth beat is characterized by a direct, purposeful move. The eleventh and twelfth beats are achieved by gentle rebounding.

Conduct exercises similar to those suggested for previous conducting patterns.

Additional Practice Problems

Your skill in conducting patterns must develop into habitual response. Preoccupation with arm direction will impede your progress as a choral interpreter. This is particularly noticeable when beginning conductors become confused about the direction their arm should move for the second beat of a three pattern versus a four pattern. A good way to develop habitual response is to conduct alternating metrical patterns. Conduct the following changing meters at a moderate tempo. Practice until you can move smoothly through them:

1. $\frac{2}{4}$ $\frac{3}{4}$ $\frac{4}{4}$ $\frac{3}{4}$ $\frac{2}{4}$

2. $\frac{6}{4}$ $\frac{12}{4}$ $\frac{3}{4}$ $\frac{12}{4}$ $\frac{6}{4}$

3. $\frac{4}{4}$ $\frac{5}{4}$ $\frac{1}{4}$ $\frac{4}{4}$ $\frac{5}{4}$

The next changing meters are to be conducted at a fast tempo. Use the following conducting patterns:

$\frac{3}{8}$—the one pattern

$\frac{6}{8}$—the two pattern

$\frac{9}{8}$—the three pattern

$\frac{12}{8}$—the four pattern

1. $\frac{3}{8}$ $\frac{6}{8}$ $\frac{3}{8}$ $\frac{9}{8}$ $\frac{3}{8}$ $\frac{12}{8}$ $\frac{3}{8}$

2. $\frac{6}{8}$ $\frac{3}{8}$ $\frac{6}{8}$ $\frac{9}{8}$ $\frac{6}{8}$ $\frac{12}{8}$ $\frac{6}{8}$

3. $\frac{12}{8}$ $\frac{3}{8}$ $\frac{12}{8}$ $\frac{6}{8}$ $\frac{12}{8}$ $\frac{9}{8}$ $\frac{12}{8}$

CONTROLLING AND MODIFYING PATTERNS

Just as the preparatory beat conditions performers for their initial attack, an additional gesture is needed for controlled cutoffs of tone.

The Release

The release can be achieved by moving the right arm and hand in a clear downward motion followed by a quick rebound. The gesture should begin one beat before the actual cutoff is to occur. Figure 4–10 shows how this downward movement occurs at the point of the conducting pattern where the actual release is to occur.

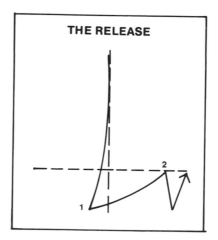

THE RELEASE

Figure 4–10

The size and force of the cutoff will depend on the mood of the music as well as the ensemble's size. Practice releases on all beats of various patterns by looking at yourself in a mirror and singing "tah" until the moment of release.

The Fermata

A fermata indicates that a pitch (or chord) is to be held for an indefinite length of time. Generally, the duration will be longer than the written note. The exact length should be based on factors such as style and the inherent dramatic qualities of the music. (See Chapter 11 for a discussion of fermata treatment.)

A slight ritard often precedes the fermata, requiring a slowing down of the conducting pattern. The beat *preceding* the fermata should be slightly increased in size to alert singers of the upcoming fermata.

Movement *during* the fermata beat is dependent on what follows. If a cutoff is to occur, the arm and hand should be held still until the release is initiated. However, if the tempo resumes immediately after the fermata, you should *slowly* move your arm and hand into position to continue with the next stroke.

NOTE: If the held note is followed by a change in tempo, a preparatory beat at the new speed must be initiated at the end of the fermata.

Conduct the following exercises at a moderate tempo, making sure to avoid abrupt movement during the fermatas:

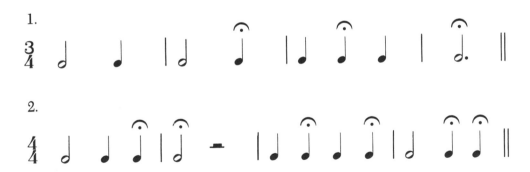

Subdivision

When the tempo of a musical work is very slow, it becomes necessary to subdivide the beats within a conducting pattern to maintain sufficient control of the ensemble. Subdivision is also essential when slowing the tempo for a ritardando or allargando. Figure 4–11 shows how to divide a three-beat pattern. The first beat is characterized by a direct, purposeful move, the second part of the first beat is achieved by gentle rebounding of the wrist and hand. The second and third beats are similarly subdivided. Practice all of the basic patterns previously learned employing subdivision technique.

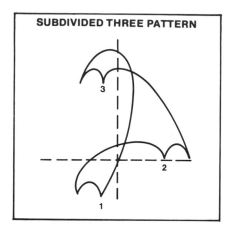

Figure 4–11

USING THE LEFT HAND

As a general rule, the left hand should not be used to mimic patterns conducted with the right hand. The left hand is essential for functions such as cueing as well as controlling dynamics and changes in tempo. During moments where the left hand is not being actively used for these functions, it should be kept at a ready position in front of the body.

Cueing

Performers are prepared for musical action by cues. Sometimes a simple head nod or eye contact is sufficient to indicate an entrance by an individual vocal section. Usually, however, a distinct cue with the left hand is necessary to ensure a confident entry by your singers. The beginning of a musical work should always be cued by the left hand in conjunction with the right hand's preparatory beat.

Left hand cues must be prepared. One beat before the actual cue, the hand should be lifted to chest height. The actual cue is characterized by a direct, purposeful move downward and slightly forward. I find it useful to keep my thumb and index finger joined during the preparatory move and suddenly opened at the moment of entry by the performers. Keep in mind that the cue *must* be directed toward the appropriate sections. This is achieved by *looking* at the singers involved slightly *before* the entrance is to occur.

Practice the following exercises, first with only the left hand, then in conjunction with the right hand beat patterns:

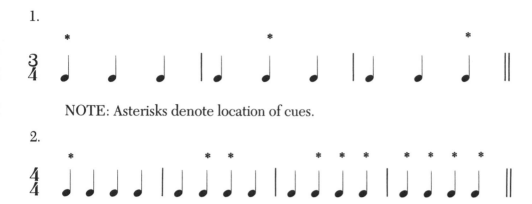

NOTE: Asterisks denote location of cues.

NOTE: Practice the same kind of exercises using the other beat patterns.

Dynamics

As was previously mentioned, the right hand beat pattern can be enlarged to communicate a louder dynamic level and decreased to show softer levels of volume. However, the left hand offers more clarity and should also be used. A crescendo is indicated by slowly lifting the left arm upward and outward with the palm up. A decrescendo is achieved by slowly lowering the left arm downward and inward with the palm down. Care must be taken to avoid abrupt movements, unless indicated by sudden changes in dynamics.

Balancing dynamics between one vocal section and another is also achieved using the above procedures. However, the appropriate gesture is directed toward a specific vocal section and reinforced by eye contact.

Changes in Tempo

The establishment of a *new* tempo within a musical work requires clarity, precision, and psychological reinforcement for the performers. The first two ingredients are achieved with the right hand, the last one with the left hand by mimicking the beat pattern until the new tempo is established.

As was previously mentioned, ritardandos and allargandos are controlled by employing subdivision of the beat pattern. At these moments I have found the left hand to be useful in mimicking the pattern.

NOTE: Remember, the left hand moves in the *opposite* direction from the right hand except for downbeats and vertical upbeats.

CHAPTER 5

DEVELOPING EXPRESSIVE CONDUCTING TECHNIQUES

The purpose of this chapter will be to discuss more advanced techniques useful for developing expressive conducting.

SHAPING PATTERNS AND GESTURES

The techniques developed for conducting orchestras during the early eighteenth century have had a profound influence on our present-day choral methods. As composers turned to the metrical system, with its measures and recurring accents, orchestra conductors turned to time beating.

Much of our choral repertoire, however, falls stylistically into periods where such an approach goes against the music's temporal and phrasal construction. For example, vocal ensemble music from the fifteenth and sixteenth centuries is often based on the *tactus*, a fixed system of *unaccented* beats. And contemporary choral music is sometimes characterized by sweeping phrases which, while notated in multi-metrical measures, should be approached as free-flowing musical sentences.

In cases where metrical construction is emphasized, such as in perpetual motion, martial-like, or strict waltz music, emphasis of the downbeat may be helpful. Generally speaking, however, choral conducting is diametrically opposed to time beating. There are two important reasons for this. (See Situation 5–A.)

- Abrupt time beating tends to fragment the music.
- "Percussive elbows," usually the result of such beating, are aesthetically incompatible with most choral music.

Conducting with Compatibility

Choral conducting, if viewed as an artistic endeavor as well as a skillful technique, must have the flexibility to accommodate the "personality" of each work. Therefore, you should not rely on rigid patterns or "stock gestures" such as "the upbeat twitch." Peter Paul Fuchs eloquently refers to flexible, compatible technique as "harmonious gesturing."[1]

There are essentially three ways to modify conducting patterns to accommodate musical character:

- By melding
- By modifying the horizontal and vertical elements of the pattern
- By employing passive gestures

SITUATION 5–A

Janet Y. complained that her singers often sang with a "tense tone." I noticed she usually conducted with a jerky motion. When she smoothed out her technique, the ensemble began to perform with less tightness and throatiness.

Melding

The first step in becoming an expressive conductor is to utilize melding patterns where applicable. This fluid technique is characterized by smooth arm and hand movement through the points of a pattern without the creation of any accent. Melding helps to achieve the following musical results:

- It encourages legato singing.
- It promotes a sense of linear melodic direction.
- It sustains musical arc.

According to Elizabeth Green, "The melded gesture is the very soul of phrasal conducting."[2]

The meld is best achieved by treating the points of the conducting pattern as imaginary circles or wheels. By maintaining a smooth, steady

---

[1]Peter Paul Fuchs, *The Psychology of Conducting* (New York: MCA Music, A Division of MCA, Inc., 1969), p. 75.

[2]Elizabeth A. H. Green, *The Modern Conductor* (Englewood Cliffs: Prentice-Hall, Inc., 1965), p. 239.

motion between and around these points, you ensure a controlled meld. (See Figure 5–1.)

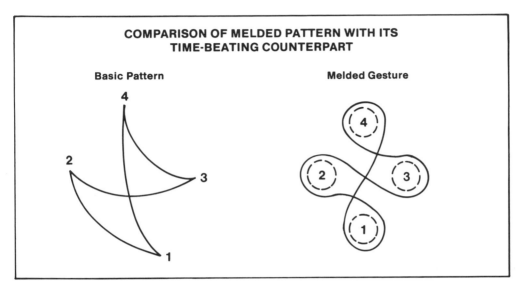

COMPARISON OF MELDED PATTERN WITH ITS TIME-BEATING COUNTERPART

Basic Pattern   Melded Gesture

Figure 5–1

Modifying Horizontal and Vertical Elements of the Pattern

With the exception of one-beat-to-the-measure gestures, conventional patterns are comprised of horizontal and vertical elements called strokes.

- The initial downward stroke represents the primary accent of the measure.
- A horizontal stroke, which moves from the conductor's left to his right *across* an imaginary vertical axis, represents the secondary accent.
- "Filler strokes" represent the remaining beats in the measure.

If the accent strokes are exaggerated, metrical structure will be emphasized. As was previously mentioned, however, most choral music does not depend on such recurrent accentuation. The use of the melded gesture is an excellent method for minimizing metrical accent.

Stress, not to be confused with accent, differs with each musical composition, depending on the work's prevailing dynamic level, performing forces, and texture. One important way to regulate this general level of weight is by modifying the overall height or breadth of the conducting pattern. (See Figure 5–2.)

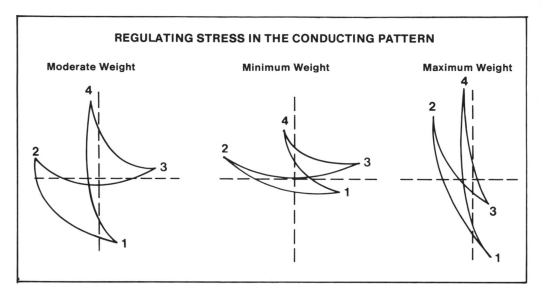

Figure 5–2

- By flattening the pattern, you minimize stress.
- By heightening the pattern, you maximize stress.

Usually you will want to enhance the music's stress tendency. For example, Paul Hindemith's delicate chanson "La Biche" ("The Doe") would be conducted with a relatively flattened pattern, modified slightly toward a more moderate height for the initial agogic accents and the contrasting forte section.

Sometimes, however, you may want to choose a contrasting type of modified pattern to achieve a more complex effect. J. S. Bach's opening "Kyrie" in his *Mass in B Minor* serves as a case in point. Although the movement is massive and weighty in its approach, the use of a flattened pattern will help to bring out its polyphonic structure. By emphasizing the linear aspect, you can avoid an overly ponderous interpretation.

O BONE JESU

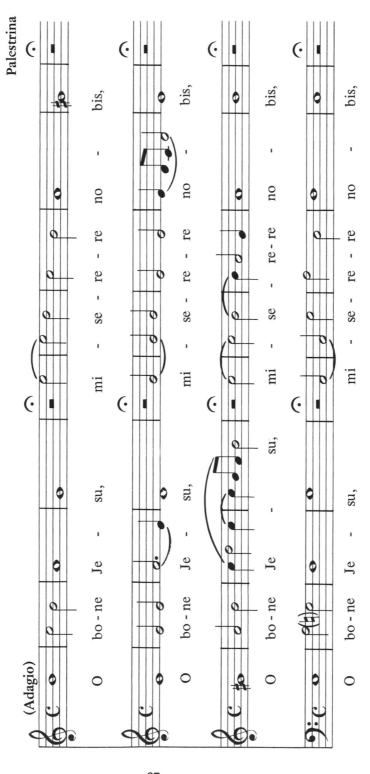

Figure 5-3

Employing Passive Gestures

Generally speaking, individual points of the conducting pattern, whether melded or articulated, must have clarity for the performer. But there are many instances in music where *all* performers hold a note for more than one beat. In such places it is best to move through the linked beat without communicating any accent, impulse, or expression. This motion is called passive gesturing. To clarify this, let us look at the opening section of Palestrina's motet, *O Bone Jesu*. (See Figure 5–3.) An analysis of each measure of this example from a conducting pattern standpoint reveals the following:

- Measure 1 should be conducted with an initially *active* downbeat followed by *passive* gesturing throughout the remainder of the pattern.

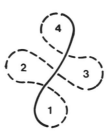

Figure 5–3A

- Measure 2 requires an active downbeat and third beat. Beats 2 and 4 are passive.

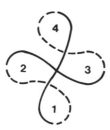

Figure 5–3B

- Measure 3 requires active motion for beats 1, 2, and 4. Beat 3 is passive.

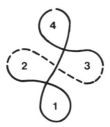

Figure 5–3C

- Measure 4 requires active motion for the first three beats because of the busy tenor line.

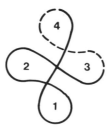

Figure 5–3D

- Measure 5 requires only an incomplete pattern beginning with beat 3 and passively moving through beat 4 because of the held rest.

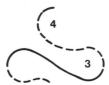

Figure 5–3E

- Measure 6 requires a continuation of passive movement which began on beat 4 of the preceding measure. Only beat 3 is active in this measure.

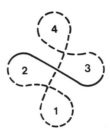

Figure 5–3F

- Measure 7 requires active movement for every beat because of a syncopated tenor line.

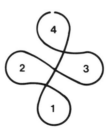

Figure 5–3G

- Measure 8 should be conducted like measure 4.
- Measure 9 requires only a downbeat followed by a delayed release. This final repose should be treated as a chord of indefinite length.

Developing Left-Hand Independence

The left hand should by no means be limited to the role of cueing. Although conducting patterns can be modified with the right hand in an effort to approximate the character of the music more closely, the *left hand* is the most important factor in developing expressive conducting.

The development of left hand communication and sense of timing must ultimately be worked out with the ensemble. Through repetition of gestures and verbalization of intention by the choral director, the singers become accustomed to his gestures and intended meaning. The left hand performs two basic expressive functions:

- Shading
- Shaping

Shading refers to the control of dynamics, intensity, and articulation. An observation of left hand movements used by various choral conductors reveals several basic shading gestures which appear to convey consistently similar meaning for most singers. (See Figure 5–4.) Singers are not only affected by the *type* of left hand movement but also by its *rate of action*. For example, a slower move creates a relatively conservative response, whereas a sudden, sharp move creates a more lively reaction.

LEFT-HAND MOVEMENT DYNAMICS

Movement	Psychological Effect	Musical Message
Downward	Quieting	Sing softer
Upward	Climactic	Sing louder
Side-to-side	Smoothing	Maintain same dynamics
Palm out	Restrictive	Controlled intensity
Palm in	Permissive	Project intensity
Angular	Disruptive	Percussive articulation
Circular	Continuity	Legato articulation

Figure 5–4

Shaping refers to the use of the left hand to lead and control melodic flow. Such gesturing demands complete diversification and independence of one hand from the other, achieved primarily through practice after patterns have become second nature. Shaping can give melodic line a sense of direction, plasticity, and momentum. Because of the creative nature of shaping, the possibilities of specific gestures are almost limitless. Here are some typical examples:

- Circular movement of the index finger to carry the ensemble through a particular spot

- Slow arc with the entire arm to depict the arsis of a phrase
- High-held hand moved lightly from side to side to suggest a flexible, transparent melodic line

WORKING WITH SINGERS

It is a significant fact that singers respond differently to various conductors. In my experiences as a conducting instructor I never cease to be amazed at the wide latitude of responses elicited from *the same choral ensemble* by beginning students. Clearly, the choral conductor's physical communication has a direct influence on the mood and quality of choral response. The reasons for this become apparent when we examine the idiosyncracies of vocal performance.

1. *The singer is both instrument and performer.* This is a unique phenomenon—it means that the instrument has feelings!

2. *The act of making music vocally results from an intimate combination of neuromuscular and psychological activity.* The singer cannot directly control the operation of the larynx. It responds *indirectly* to signals sent from the brain. For example, a violinist controls pitch by sliding his or her fingers up and down the strings. A singer *thinks* the pitch, then depends on the brain to send the proper signal to the larynx. The element of psychology obviously plays an important role in conditioning this signal. An intimidated singer may have difficulty in performing a high note because of a perceived risk.

3. *The vocalist sings "from the inside out."* Singing is an energized process which originates deep down inside. The emission of air to produce a vocal tone is regulated by interplay between the diaphragm and the intercostal muscles. The airstream then flows past the vocal folds in the larynx, where it becomes transformed into tonal energy. Finally, it travels through various cavities in the head where it is colored, amplified, and given textual meaning. The degree and nature of this action will be directly influenced by the way you conduct your patterns. Some examples are:
   - Conducting with a "flapping" motion will incur relatively weak tone from your singers.
   - Conducting a pattern close to your abdominal area will tend to produce a well-supported tone.

Singers respond especially well to a conductor whose patterns appear to "draw out" the vocal tones.

"Drawing Power"

"Drawing power" is best achieved by *pulling* the lower part of the arm through the conducting pattern. As you may know, many muscles in the body work together in pairs. Arm movements are controlled by an interaction between the bicep (in the upper arm) and the forcep (in the lower arm). By pulling the lower arm *against* slight resistance in the upper arm, you will achieve a *controlled intensity* in your conducting patterns. This will give you "drawing power," resulting in energized vocal response. This effect can be achieved by pretending to conduct patterns underwater.

EXPRESSION THROUGH BODY LANGUAGE

Kinesics—The Science of Nonverbal Communication

Kinesics is a field of study which has exciting implications for the conducting profession. This science is concerned with ways that humans send messages to one another through facial expression, arm and hand movements, and posturing. According to experts in the field, people employ physical behavioral patterns, which are partly learned and partly instinctive, to communicate such basic feelings as hate, fear, joy, and sadness.

Successful choral conductors, perhaps without realizing it, are usually sophisticated body language communicators. Besides achieving technically secure ensemble results through traditional gesturing, they are able to establish contrasting musical moods and elicit a more total effort from singers. Their success results from a capacity to physically show feeling for a musical composition and an ability to communicate their performance demands while conducting.

Avoiding Masking and Shielding

As children grow into adulthood, they begin to build defense mechanisms for protection from society's unwanted intrusions. *Masking* and *shielding* are two basic types of physical defense. The first step in developing skill as a nonverbal communicator is to learn how to avoid these restrictive mechanisms when you are working with choral ensembles.

1. *Masking* refers to the practice of immobilizing facial expression so that emotion or feeling is not conveyed. However, the possibilities in facial communication are too important to overlook. Creating mood for the music at hand through countenance, encouraging singers at points of entry with the eyes, and prolonging alertness and vitality through personal demeanor are

just a few examples of utilizing conducive facial expression. (See Situation 5–B).

Sometimes conductors unconsciously convey the wrong facial message because of their unawareness of this communicative vehicle. For example, by visually reacting to misinterpreted notes during a performance, the choral leader runs the risk of creating a pessimistic feeling among ensemble members. Smiling, while usually beneficial, is sometimes out of place and can detrimentally affect the concert mood. Peter Paul Fuchs observes,

> There is nothing more offensive and disillusioning than a conductor who, after the sublimely ethereal final chords of Mahler's *Lied von der Erde*, takes his bow with a broad grin on his face.[3]

SITUATION 5–B

Danielle V's choral concerts always generate excitement. When asked why they sing with such enthusiasm, her singers exclaim, "We can tell by her face she expects great things from us."

The following exercise will help you to develop facial expressivity: Imagine that you are conducting choral works which deal with the following topics:

- Gypsies dancing to a merry tune (Mood—gaiety)
- A funeral procession (Mood—solemnity)
- Soldiers marching to victory (Mood—bravery)
- A father seeking revenge for his murdered daughter (Mood—anger)

For each example look at yourself in the mirror to see if you can reveal the appropriate mood through facial expression. Consider the following possibilities as you experiment:

- Smiling
- Frowning
- Squinting your eyes

---

[3]Fuchs, op. cit. p. 75.

- Wrinkling your forehead
- Glaring with your eyes
- Staring
- Pouting
- Showing your teeth
- Wrinkling your nose

2. *Body shielding* refers to the act of limiting general body movements and gesturing to practical necessity. Yet anyone who has seen the famous mime Marcel Marceau realizes how expressively communicative the body can be. Partly because of Puritan-based influences, the use of the body for expression other than in dancing has been relatively restricted in our country.

In choral performance this indispensable expressive resource is best employed to *set an example*. Some ways conductors use this power of suggestion to get results are

- Encouraging singers to support their tonal production by conducting with the chest held high
- Suggesting robust sonority by opening the leg stance
- Enhancing the performance of coloratura phrases by raising the height of the entire conducting pattern

On a more advanced level the application of physical demonstration transforms the choral director's role into what Wilhelm Ehmann calls a "Symbolic dancer." He refers to the importance of keeping alive a sense of "inner dancing" among the members of a choral ensemble. And the author envisions the conductor as a co-participant who "never dances 'the whole dance'. . . . He makes only his hands and his arms dance—the rest of him being kept on the brink of dancing without yielding to the impulse."[4]

Developing Body Language Through Empathy

The word "empathy" was originally used by psychologists and refers to an individual's capacity to understand others through insight and feeling. As used by many musicians, it has come to mean a feeling of cohesion between

---

[4]Wilhelm Ehmann, *Choral Directing*, Trans. George D. Wiebe (Minneapolis: Augsburg Publishing House, 1968), p. 167.

the conductor and each performer and among the members of the ensemble. Empathy can, and should, exist between sections of the ensemble as well. (See Figure 5–5.)

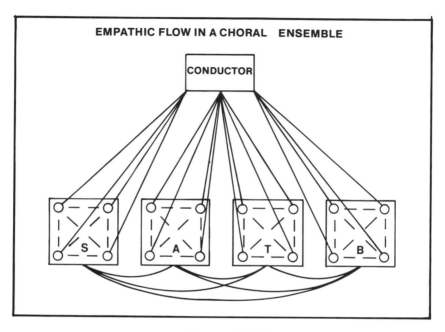

Figure 5–5

In empathizing with our singers, we must learn to stimulate them *through body language* so that they will perform with the proper energizing action necessary to achieve the best vocal result. By working with the ensemble, we must find ways to "pull" the music out of the performer. One concept which seems particularly helpful in this regard is described as follows:

> The choral director should develop the constant image that he or she is connected by *several* strings to each member of the ensemble. Whenever hands, arms, or chest are moved, there should be a *physical* feeling of directly controlling the singer's response.

In other words, we must develop an intimate performance rapport with our singers. This link must be established before we make music and is achieved by first looking around at the members to establish eye contact.

THE CHORAL CONDUCTOR AND THE ORCHESTRA

The choral director who hopes to work successfully with instrumentalists must learn to communicate with them in a somewhat different way than with singers. This difference becomes evident when one considers the orchestral musician's background. The proficient instrumentalist has usually spent many years attempting to master an instrument and learning to sight-read. And, as a result of this discipline, he or she tends to approach performance as an artistic craftsperson. Singers also seek technical proficiency, but they are generally more dependent on group motivation and extramusical factors than their instrumental colleagues.

The orchestral musician usually expects clear, concise instructions and accurate accounting for measures by the conductor. If there is such a thing as "The Golden Rule of Orchestral Conducting," it would undoubtedly be stated as follows:

Always maintain a clear downbeat for every measure!

The history of orchestral performance is full of instances in which wrong entrances occurred because the conductor failed to maintain metrical integrity.

Some Guidelines for Directing the Instrumental Ensemble

Competent instrumentalists have learned to count fast and efficiently. Be prepared to work at a relatively faster rehearsal pace. Here are some suggestions.

1. Be ready to offer suggestions to string players about bowing and articulation. Consult a string player, if necessary, for this information.

2. If *potential* trouble spots involve transposing instruments, study these parts closely so that pitch problems can be remedied effectively.

3. For works of extended length use well-placed rehearsal letters rather than measure numbers. Mark the distances from these letters at which important activity occurs.

4. Check instrumentalists' parts for inconvenient page turns and provide additional parts or written-out inserts if necessary.

One of the most challenging problems for those fortunate enough to have the service of a large instrumental ensemble is to remember individual locations of instruments so that they may be properly cued. Usually,

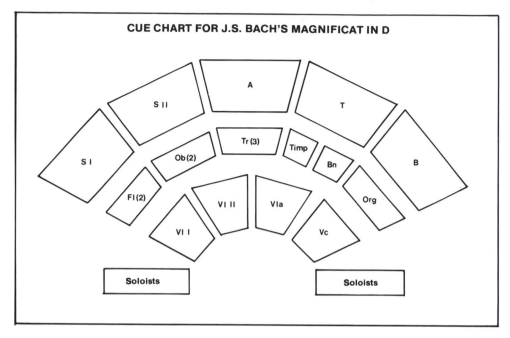

Figure 5–6

instrumental musicians are available for only a few rehearsals just before the concert. One aid which I have found to be particularly useful is the cue chart. After determining your seating arrangement for both the singers and the instrumentalists, plot the locations on a piece of cardboard. (See Figure 5–6.) By sitting at a desk with the cue chart positioned behind the score, you can practice cueing and ensure familiarity with locations before actual rehearsals and performances.

CHAPTER 6

CONDUCTING REHEARSALS

If I were asked to choose three ingredients for a successful choral program, I would have to narrow down my choices to the following:

- Exciting performances
- Captivating repertoire
- Vibrant rehearsals

In view of the fact that up to 90 percent of an ensemble's time is spent in rehearsals, it is paramount that these events prove to be productive and rewarding.

During my experiences as choral director and in talking with others, I have found that inferior rehearsals can be attributed to one or more of five major problem areas:

- *Lack of purpose.* Usually caused by insufficient or faulty planning
- *Boredom.* Often attributable to unrealistic pacing and lack of variety
- *Interruptions.* Created by factors such as inefficient distribution of music and repetitious explanations
- *Lack of rapport.* Results from the director's unawareness of group psychology and leadership principles
- *Underachievement.* Caused by insufficient group motivation and lack of diligence.

In this chapter we will explore the major areas necessary to ensure successful daily rehearsals.

A PLANNING GUIDE

Rehearsals should not be conceived as separate, independent sessions. Each should be planned as a link to achieving long-range goals. Chapter 2 presented the following "Areas of Development" necessary for a well-balanced choral program:

- Vocal skills
- Musical knowledge
- Musicianship
- Ensemble
- Social skills

The chapter went on to explain how goals within each area can be reached during three "Levels of Achievement"—

- Achievement Level I: Orientation
- Achievement Level II: Growth
- Achievement Level III: Culmination

It is important to keep in mind that these goals are reached while your singers are studying repertoire. In other words, Achievement Levels are reached *while preparing music for performance*.

Later in this book, I will show you how music is best prepared in three stages—

- Note learning and technical mastery
- Polishing
- Interpreting

If we align these three music preparation stages with the five "Areas of Development" previously mentioned, we can construct a "Planning Guide" for each Achievement Level. (See Figure 6–1.) Then, when we select a piece of music for a rehearsal, we can utilize the Planning Guide to determine which goals will be appropriate for the session.

The following are some examples of activities suitable for Achievement Level I:

- During the *Note Learning and Technical Mastery* stage, the dynamic markings of a new musical work could be discussed to further *Musical Knowledge*.
- During the *Polishing* stage, attacks and releases of musical phrases could be drilled to develop *Ensemble*.
- During the *Interpreting* stage, *Musicianship* could be improved by demonstrating the need to emphasize a recurring textual phrase or sequential pattern.

```
PLANNING GUIDE

* * * * * * * * * *

Achievement Level (Check one) 1. ____ 2. ____ 3. ____
```

	Note Learning and Technical Mastery	Polishing	Interpreting
Vocal skills			
Musical knowledge			
Musicianship			
Ensemble			
Social skills			

Figure 6–1

As you read through this book, you will get more ideas for useful activities. Chapter 8, "Working with Singers" will be especially helpful for planning vocal events.

COORDINATING ACTIVITIES

As a rule, choral rehearsals do not begin with heavy singing. Activities should be planned in a logical sequence. A well-organized rehearsal tends to flow through the following three phases:

- Preparation
- Execution
- Culmination

Nonmusical activities such as announcements are interspersed with performance to provide vocal rest. Figure 6–2 presents a comprehensive sequence for a specific rehearsal.

TYPICAL REHEARSAL SEQUENCE

Preparation { Physical Exercises
Mental Exercises
Vocal Exercises

Execution { Polishing of Work #1
Announcements
Polishing of Work #2
Discussion of Stage Deportment

Culmination { Application of Deportment to Works I and II
Final Remarks

Figure 6–2

Choosing Strategies

Once music has been selected, goals determined, and a sequence of events established for the regular rehearsal, you are ready to choose specific strategies to achieve desired results. For example, if your goal is to have the sopranos execute a Baroque trill properly, you may choose as a strategy to demonstrate on piano the difference between a Classical and a Baroque trill.

Visuals such as chalkboard diagrams of forms can also be used effectively. Chapters 8 through 11 contain many strategies useful for achieving vocal, music learning, and performance goals. Use the following list of action verbs when developing your strategies:[1]

- Show
- Discuss
- Manipulate
- Imitate
- Compare
- Describe
- Define

- Identify
- Classify
- Modify
- Rearrange
- Reshape
- Vary
- Combine

_____

[1]Bennett Reimer, *A Philosophy of Music Education* (Englewood Cliffs: Prentice-Hall, 1970), p. 121.

- Contrast
- Develop
- Inspect
- Observe
- Amplify
- Reconstruct
- Characterize
- Infer
- Disclose

- Clarify
- Demonstrate
- Explain
- Appraise
- Discuss
- Recall
- Locate
- Invent

A Daily Rehearsal Plan

The following ingredients are necessary for consistently superior rehearsals:

- The director knows "where the group is coming from"
- The director knows "where the group needs to go"
- The director has a clear idea of what needs to be accomplished in each rehearsal

Information already provided in this chapter as well as in Chapter 2 will assist you with the first two ingredients. Figure 6–3 presents a "Daily Rehearsal Plan" useful for aligning strategies with objectives already determined in the Planning Guide. Other items such as "Announcements" are included. Once the plan is completed, you need to determine your sequence of events. (See Situation 6–A.)

SITUATION 6–A

Mary M. was good at choosing choral ensemble goals and organizing activities. Yet students complained that her rehearsals were "plodding and boring." A visiting director noted that her strategies were often ineffective. She attended workshops to develop better strategies. Now her rehearsals are viewed by her students as "fun and rewarding."

DAILY REHEARSAL PLAN

EXERCISES:	Objectives	Strategies
Physical		
Mental Preparation		
Vocal		

REPERTOIRE:	Objectives	Strategies
1.		
2.		
3.		

SUPPLEMENTAL AND CULMINATING ACTIVITIES:	Objectives	Strategies
1.		
2.		

SPECIAL RESOURCES:

Figure 6–3

ESTABLISHING STANDARD OPERATING PROCEDURES

The rehearsal may be well planned, but its effectiveness will depend on the way in which activities are presented and conducted. Overly methodical rehearsals fail to generate a feeling of spontaneity and enthusiasm. On the other hand, guidelines are necessary to facilitate smooth and efficient operation (Situation 6–B).

SITUATION 6–B

Gary F. complained that he had discipline problems with his singers. When I attended one of his rehearsals, I noticed he would have individual vocal sections sing through an entire selection while others waited—and talked! I pointed out that he should use the sectional approach only for short periods. I also showed him how to get others involved by singing lightly on "loo loo" or clapping the rhythm.

Rehearsal Principles

Successful leaders learn to recognize "fundamental laws" within their profession which can be violated only at risk. What would be your reaction to a football coach who never allowed his team to punt the ball on a fourth down? Rehearsals are also subject to several principles. Do not overlook them for other than exceptional reasons.

1. *Begin and end the rehearsal with high-interest repertoire.* After the initial exercises have been completed, move right into music you know will produce an enthusiastic response. Save announcements until later when the singers will also benefit from a short rest. End the rehearsal by performing for enjoyment a work which the ensemble has been meticulously preparing. This will allow them to appreciate their efforts. Or choose a previously learned work which they particularly like.

2. *Plan for variety in activities.* Singers become bored when they are required to work too long on one choral selection. This is especially true when conductors attempt to accomplish note learning, polishing, and interpreting of a single composition all at once. When you are rehearsing a major work, move through several sections, perhaps even out of normal order, to achieve variety.

3. *Keep singers invigorated.* Did you know that the imminence of bad weather (falling barometric pressure) causes poor singing? High humidity also has a detrimental effect on intonation. But, despite

these problems, or even complacent ensemble response, the show must go on. Here are four ways to invigorate your singers:

- Keep the group on its toes with surprises such as unexpected changes in tempo, delayed cues, or key changes.
- Tell a joke or capitalize on humorous situations which develop in rehearsal.
- Alternate between group sitting and standing. Get people moving, even while they are singing.
- Plan for breaks or short intermissions when you are rehearsing for longer than one hour.

4. *Avoid vocal strain.* Intersperse lighter, more lyrical selections with heavier, declamatory works. Loud passages may be sung at a more moderate dynamic level until notes are learned. Is it necessary for the sopranos to hold that high G for thirteen beats every time you rehearse "America the Beautiful?"

5. *Establish a realistic pace.* Let's face it, some days are "off days" for your ensemble. In other instances you may have set standards which are unrealistic for a new choral situation. If, in spite of your efforts, you cannot reach planned objectives, be prepared to settle for what you can get. As a rule, try to set and maintain a realistic pace by keeping no more or less than one step ahead of your performers at all times.

6. *Make efficient use of time.* Any instance in which a singer is not engaged in some form of musical activity is a waste of time. Do not expect a vocal section to sit and watch you rehearse others for more than five minutes. Plan sectional rehearsals or stagger the arrival and departure of individual sections if you must rehearse a section for a long period of time. Good choral rehearsals can be characterized as musically purposeful; poor rehearsals are disruptive.

Mechanics of Operation

All organizations adopt procedures so that they may function as smoothly as possible on an everyday basis. Experience has shown that certain mechanics of operation are necessary for an efficient choral rehearsal.

1. *Establish a method for distributing music.* Each singer should be assigned a music number for accountability. By spreading new music

(in numerical order) across a table near the entrance to the rehearsal room, you can save valuable time. Another method is to have two helpers pass around music as they call singers' numbers in tandem.

2. *Get each choral member into the habit of using a pencil.* Singers are usually very optimistic about their ability to remember all of the information you provide about changes in the music. Slowed rehearsals and occasional memory lapses in performance have proven otherwise.

3. *Give musical locations with precision.* "Begin on page seven, the fourth brace, the second measure, the third beat." Repeat the location and then promptly begin. When you are referring to locations strictly by rehearsal letters or numbers, try to resume at these designators. If you must begin at a place in between, use the following format: "From rehearsal letter (or number) X count forward (or backward) with me." Then proceed to count out loud as you move toward the spot at which you plan to begin.

4. *Establish a standard procedure for handling divisi choral scoring.* Designate individual singers to perform specific parts whenever the scoring expands from its normal pattern.

5. *Coordinate rehearsal plans with accompanists.* As a minimal courtesy, they should be told in advance which choral selections you plan to rehearse so that they may practice. Other useful information would include the following:

- Initial rehearsal and final concert tempos
- Difficult choral phrases requiring demonstration by the accompanist
- How you intend to conduct passages requiring close musical coordination

If new exercises are to be introduced, show the accompanist how you intend to execute them.

SEATING ARRANGEMENTS

Many choral directors use the basic "ducks in a row" sectional seating arrangement with higher voices in front for all rehearsals and concerts. Yet there are circumstances when this configuration actually works *against* the ensemble. (See Situation 6–C.)

SITUATION 6–C

Allen H. had a "muddy, plodding" bass section in his men's glee club. When he placed the brighter sounding tenors behind them, the basses began to "come alive" vocally and rhythmically.

Formations for rehearsing and performing should be based on the following factors:

1. *Number of singers.* When large ensembles are arranged by sections, it may be easier to control balances, mold individual lines, and give specific cues. On the other hand, the mixed-quartet or "scrambled" format may work better for chamber-sized groups where overall group blend becomes a premium consideration.

2. *Balance between vocal parts.* If you have relatively few tenors in a mixed group, it would be better to place them as an integrated section in front. In a girl's chorus, by spacing second sopranos behind first sopranos and altos you can "splinter them off" to achieve better balance during two-part singing.

3. *Ability of singers.* Less-experienced singers usually learn more quickly and feel more secure when placed in sections. Conversely, a "scrambled" arrangement develops a stronger sense of ensemble between seasoned individuals.

4. *Contrasts between individual singers.* Placement of individuals, even within sections, should also be considered. One school of thought is to put stronger, more confident singers in back so that their voices will carry through the ensemble. Another line of thinking is to juxtapose stronger with weaker voices, experienced with "rookie" singers, excellent with mediocre readers, etc. Vocal *qualities* should also be considered. Heavy voices may be placed next to those with a lighter quality. Avoid placing strident voices together, or you will compound their harshness.

5. *Structure of the music.* Studies show audiences prefer a sectional format when listening to contrapuntal (imitative) music; they can hear the semi-independent performance of each section in "stereophonic relief." They like a mixed-chorus arrangement for homophonic (chordal) performance because they hear a more cohesive sound.

6. *Appearance.* Height needs to be considered as well for lines of sight and overall appearance. A small male section can at least be *visually* balanced in a mixed choir by flanking them with larger soprano and alto sections.

Suggestions for Seating Configurations

1. Whenever possible, use a semicircle. This allows performers to sing more to each other and to hear better. According to Wilhelm Ehmann,

   > The advantages of the half-circle formation are realized in the closer contact of the singers with each other; it permits the director to be placed in line with the stream of sound and is conducive to the development of good sonority.[2]

2. At first, stay with one seating arrangement. New singers need time to adjust to ways of doing things. Other formations should be introduced later when procedures and activities have been established.

3. Establish a final arrangement several rehearsals before concert. Singers need to become accustomed to their surroundings. It is important that they have time to adjust vocally to others around them.

4. Consider using an alternating seating plan as follows:
   - For the note-learning and technical mastery stage use the sectional plan to secure pitches and build initial confidence in performing new music.
   - For the polishing stage switch to the mixed-quartet arrangement to develop musical interplay between singers. I also like to use other formats such as a circle or circles within circles to increase empathy.
   - For the interpreting stage return to the original plan to refine sectional contributions.

5. Allow for adequate spacing between singers. Remember, a cramped ensemble produces a *smaller* sound.

The following plans have been used successfully to achieve their intended results:

---

[2]Wilhelm Ehmann, *Choral Directing*, Trans. George D. Wiebe (Minneapolis: Augsburg Publishing House, 1968), p. 8.

1. Weak men's sections

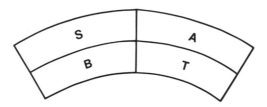

Figure 6–4

NOTE: Placing extreme ranges behind each other improves tuning and blending.

2. Fewer men than women

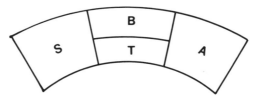

Figure 6–5

3. SATB to SS^2ATT^2B within a work or program

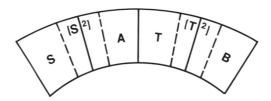

Figure 6–6

4. Use of an echo choir on stage

Figure 6–7

5. Antiphonal arrangement between two similar-sized choirs

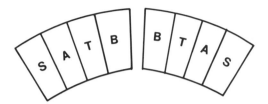

Figure 6–8

6. Projection of theme in cantus firmus types of compositions

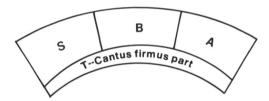

Figure 6–9

7. Overpowering sopranos and tenors

Figure 6–10

8. Scrambled

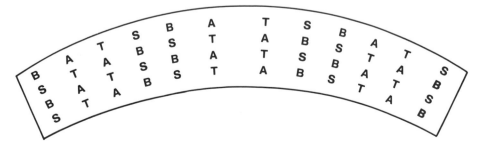

Figure 6–11

9. Modified scrambled to preserve sectional support from rear to front

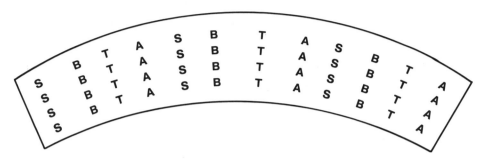

Figure 6–12

CHAPTER   7

MOTIVATING THE ENSEMBLE

Of all the nonmusical skills necessary for successful choral directing, the ability to motivate ensemble members toward rehearsal and performance goals is probably the most important. This proficiency is only developed through knowledge of human behavior and practical experience in working with people. Your success will be directly dependent on the following factors:

- Your ability to perceive individual and group needs
- A realistic understanding of your own attributes and limitations as a leader-motivator
- Your insight or feel for human relations
- Your effectiveness in managing interpersonal relationships and influencing human events

SOME FACTS ABOUT PEOPLE AND GROUPS

Choral directors are judged to a large extent by their ability to produce quality ensembles. Sometimes it is possible to forget that organizations are molded from individuals whose efforts and abilities ultimately determine the group's success. Human beings are sensitive to the nature of their leader's persuasion. If manipulated, they can become obstinate; if inspired, they will sacrifice.

The Individual Singer

As a member of an ensemble the singer has basic needs which must be satisfied. Here are some examples:

1. The individual seeks to maintain his or her identity within a group situation. The use of a nickname or preference for unusual or distinctive clothes are indications of this need for individuality. Holding a "Meet the Singers" session during the first rehearsal of the season is a great way to discover the unique interests and experiences of your members.

117

2. New singers have a need to be accepted by the ensemble. The strength of this need varies from mild concern to total preoccupation depending on such factors as self-confidence, previous experiences, and stature of the group. An orientation, whether in the form of a short discussion period for each singer or as a formal meeting for an entire contingent of performers, is effective for integrating new members into the choral organization. Holding an informal social event like a party is also excellent for breaking the ice for new singers.

3. Individuals like to feel that their contribution is necessary for the group's success. Nothing discourages a singer more than to feel like excess baggage in a vocal ensemble. He or she must feel important, and importance means responsibility. You can help your members to find satisfaction as contributors in two ways:

   • By emphasizing the "link in the chain" theory and challenging all to fulfill their responsibilities
   • By personally letting individuals know that their contributions are appreciated ("Thanks for helping me and the group").

   Sometimes it is difficult for a singer to feel effective as a member of a 150-voice chorus. One way to recognize contribution in such a large organization is by presenting awards for attendance. (See Situation 7–A.)

SITUATION 7–A

Emma K. lives in Germany where she is a faithful member of the local *Liederkranz*. She takes pride in her gradually increasing collection of wine glasses awarded each year for perfect attendance in the singing group.

---

4. Individuals are motivated by a hierarchy of needs. Singers join a choral organization because of a *general* need—to sing. However, the amount of motivation varies with each individual depending on the strength of various sub-needs and the chance to satisfy these needs. Here are some hypothetical cases which clarify this point:

   • Soprano *X* was a soloist with her former group before moving into the area. She chose your ensemble because you perform extended works requiring soloists.

- Tenor Y was always "too busy" to join the choir—until he found out the vocal group is making plans to sing at Disneyland.
- Alto Z used to be lonely and shy. She performed a solo in the last choral concert.

If you bring the individual's needs close to the group's needs, everyone will benefit. There are two ways to accomplish this goal:

- By knowing the special talents, abilities, and interests of each member and by providing opportunities for them whenever possible
- By "turning members on" to values and benefits inherent in the choral program. This process persuades individuals to adopt *new* personal needs which coincide with group needs.

5. Individuals work better in positive environments. The choral organization depends on the improvement and development of its members for success. Because this growth process involves learning, factors known as reward and punishment come into play. According to the psychologist James Coleman:

> Negative or divergent feedback . . . has the effect of punishment, but its results may vary. . . . Rewards . . . tend to reinforce what has been learned and to motivate further learning.[1]

Provide a positive environment by following a simple guideline: *Praise frequently; criticize indirectly!*

Obviously, a good choral ensemble results from a demanding director. Too much criticism, however, can be discouraging. For example, sarcastic comments may create a cynical attitude among members and even affect tone quality. Group goals can be achieved with enjoyment if you take a positive approach by *encouraging* change.

The Choral Group

Like the individual, the group can be characterized by its patterns of behavior. In fact, much insight can be gained by viewing the organization as a "collective individual."

---

[1] James C. Coleman, *Psychology and Effective Behavior* (Glenview, Illinois: Scott, Foresman and Company, 1969), p. 383.

1. The group has its own personality. This personality is determined by the following factors:
   - The organization's customs, beliefs, and values
   - The shared attitudes and motives of its members
   - The social structure of the group
   - The cohesiveness, sense of purpose, and morale of the group

   You must be receptive and adaptive to the choral ensemble's personality. What works for one group will not necessarily work for another. (See Situation 7–B.)

SITUATION 7–B

David H. left his position at a large public high school to take over the male glee club at a smaller private school. He was unable to bring his new ensemble up to expectations because he had difficulty adjusting to the group's traditions, values, and attitudes.

   This does not mean that a group's nature cannot be changed. A responsible director will always see reason to promote important values and strengthen morale. However, the practical leader will learn to discern between a group's *inherent* traits and its changeable characteristics.

2. The group's energy is affected by patterns of inertia and momentum. Anyone who has faced a tired choral ensemble on the Monday following a busy weekend tour has experienced the effects of group inertia. The reverse effect tends to take place as groups near their goals. Successful football coaches are acutely aware of this ebb-and-flow phenomenon. They attempt to preserve peak efficiency throughout the season by maintaining a demanding training program and by offering incentives such as "the sweet smell of victory."

   The best way to generate momentum and keep it is to continually provide *interesting* incentives and goals. For example, choose a lighter, novelty piece for the school ensemble's first rehearsal of the spring semester. An established church choir plagued by the duty of having to provide just one more anthem for the Sunday service might pull out of its rut by preparing for a special Saturday night secular concert. Unique concert appearances, unusual repertoire, social events, and even a change in rehearsal location are just a few examples of ways to keep the group on the move.

3. Groups tend to gravitate toward pre-established values and priorities. This is especially true of older groups in their efforts to maintain the status quo. Organizations are accommodating to their leaders as long as they emphasize the values sought by that particular group. (See Situation 7–C.)

This condition often becomes apparent when a new director attempts to change some aspect of the program and is confronted with the remark, "We used to do it another way." The introduction of new values and ideas may require tact, patience, and persistence. Often, the ability to "sell" new ways of doing things can make the difference between acceptance and rejection.

SITUATION 7–C

Two potential directors auditioned for an industrial/business chorus. The more musically adept applicant was passed over in favor of a younger neophyte. The latter's promise to provide enjoyable lunchtime recreation proved to be the deciding factor.

ESTABLISHING A VIABLE RAPPORT

It is the rare individual who can step into a new leadership position and get immediate dramatic results. Usually such changes and improvements require a certain amount of working and growing together between the leader and the group.

Establishing and maintaining a cooperative spirit is especially important in choral performance, because the director and the singers must achieve an unusually sensitive working relationship for performing vocal music. There are three important steps which you can personally take to achieve this rapport:

- Develop an environment conducive to making music.
- Establish necessary guidelines and rules.
- Observe the basic principles of leadership.

Develop an Environment Conducive to Making Music

Individuals join organizations for various reasons, some not always compatible with the main purpose of the group. The classic example of this occurs when church members join choirs so that they may be prominently seen on Sundays. Sometimes the group itself, because of wayward leadership or an unclear sense of values, reaches for its musical goals in a roundabout way. (See Situation 7–D.) Some time ago, I directed a college glee club whose student officers were preoccupied with social activities. Rehearsals were marred by high absenteeism and lack of musical purpose.

SITUATION 7–D

Carol E.'s predecessor was a church choir director who liked to joke and chat during most of each rehearsal. Needless to say, the quality of performance was mediocre. It took her several weeks to reestablish a sense of musical purpose.

Your best approach is to make it clear, through verbal communication and through action, that *musical performance* is the nucleus around which the choral program is built. Individual, group, and director interests must be molded and channelled toward that basic activity. (See Figure 7–1.)

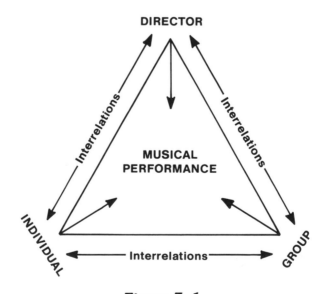

Figure 7–1

1. *Avoid "uptight" situations.* Sometimes tensions result from the pressure of inadequate rehearsal time or differences of opinion. If they are allowed to lead to feelings of hostility, the choral program will suffer. The

best way to prevent such conditions is by underplaying the apparent seriousness of the issue involved. There is usually a humorous side to every human situation.

2. *Avoid generalized criticism.* Experienced choral directors have learned that lectures to the group or censure of vocal sections rarely pay off. In such instances, singers do not often accept personal blame. Without losing tact, the director must pinpoint mistakes and make spot corrections. This approach allows everyone to make music with minimum interference.

Establish Necessary Guidelines and Rules

No organization can exist without the cooperation of its members. To unify and direct this collaborative spirit between individuals, guidelines and rules become necessary. They may be written or assumed or maintained by you or the ensemble's officers, but they must exist.

A viable rapport which allows the leader and the group to reach for essential objectives can only be established when all are willing to play the game by its rules. Sociologists have shown that groups need controls *and expect their leaders to provide them.* This does not mean that choral directors should become law enforcement officers; it simply means that healthy individual interests must be directed productively toward group goals.

The exact format and approach for establishing regulatory controls will depend on the nature of the choral organization. A military academy would tend to adopt a relatively strict code for its glee club members. An adult church choir, on the other hand, will usually respond cooperatively to a verbally presented policy. There are, however, three essential areas of group control which must be clarified for *all* choral ensembles.

1. *Punctuality.* Begin on time and end on time. This policy is based on the assumption that individuals should not be delayed by others. A sixty-voice choral ensemble which begins five minutes late does not lose five minutes. It loses sixty times five minutes or *five manpower hours.*

2. *Absenteeism.* Insist on standards of attendance. I have yet to meet a singer who did not have a good reason for missing a choral rehearsal or performance. The issue is really one of priorities. If an individual misses a rehearsal because of a 103 degree temperature, one would say that his or her sense of priority was reasonable. Conversely, if a member skips a dress rehearsal to watch a televised football game, one would obviously question this choice. The important point of this discussion is contained in the following rule:

Insist that choral group members place a high priority on attendance!

Usually, some type of quota system or regulations will be necessary. Some examples are:

- Church choir members who miss two successive rehearsals cannot sing the following Sunday.
- Attendance is mandatory for rehearsals occurring one week before concerts.
- A maximum of two absences will be allowed during the school semester.

3. *Attention.* Require active participation and concentration from all members. Individuals rarely come to a rehearsal with the intent of disrupting the group. They *do*, however, like to *talk*. Conversation must be restricted to before and after the rehearsal. The best way to keep singers "on the ball" is to give concise directions, then immediately follow up with execution. Sometimes, a simple remark like "Let's get with the action" will motivate individuals to keep attentive.

Observe the Basic Principles of Leadership

Organizations respond differently to various leaders for many reasons. One of the most important factors in choral ensemble leadership is the director's personality. Yet it is obvious that individuals with completely different lifestyles and personalities can achieve equally superior results.

While each choral director must discover which methods and approaches work best, he or she must keep in mind that a group expects certain basic considerations from its leader. The best way to establish a viable rapport is by observing the following principles of leadership:

1. *Be consistent.* A group cannot follow a straight line toward its goals if the leader vacillates in judgment. For example, if singers are allowed to sit in random order one day and are admonished for this the next day, they become confused and defensive. Yet consistency should not be confused with inflexibility or stubbornness. The person who refuses to change a decision in the face of contrary evidence is a fool.

2. *Be fair and impartial.* Do not make exceptions. "A chorus cannot tolerate exceptions for individuals: any *prima donna* treatment signifies the beginning of the end of a genuinely integrated membership."[2] Avoid

---

[2]Kurt Thomas, *The Choral Conductor*. Trans. Alfred Mann and William H. Reese. (New York: Associated Music Publishers, 1971), p. 43.

sectional favoritism or disproportionate criticism of one section over the others. If a choral ensemble is favored by an abundance of good sopranos and plagued by a dearth of tenors (a situation encountered by most directors sooner or later), partiality will obviously polarize the situation.

This discussion is not intended to suggest that individuals or sections should not be acknowledged for superior performance. Rather it means that all must know they have an equal chance to succeed. And the best way to remain fair and impartial is by *challenging* all persons and sections to reach their true potential.

3. *Be reliable.* Group standards will not be met unless the group's leader sets an example. How can a director expect ensemble members to be punctual if he or she is not? The old expression, "Do as I say, not as I do," is the banal code of inferior leaders and reflects a calloused indifference to followers.

4. *Be loyal.* Loyalty works both ways. If the group feels that its leader cares and is willing to fight for its cause, support will grow for the leader. Loyalty also means sharing the credits for success. Choral directors sometimes receive letters praising well-received performances; as a matter of professional policy, these notes should be read to the ensemble, followed by a personal "thank you."

5. *Be decisive.* The ability to solve problems and make decisions is not always easy to acquire, but it is a responsibility of leadership. Groups may like "nice guys," but they respect decision-makers. (See Situation 7–E.)

SITUATION 7–E

Gordon P. was faced with the task of choosing members for a select university chamber choir. Of those singers returning for audition, two were not asked to rejoin the group. This decision was based on a preference for two more talented freshmen and a desire to maintain a continual flow of new members. Although the "retired" singers expressed personal disappointment, members in the newly formed chamber choir were able to establish a tighter rapport and perform better than last year's group.

---

6. *Keep everyone informed.* No one likes to be "left out in the cold" about group plans and activities. Obviously, individuals will work better toward group objectives if they are continually kept abreast of all decisions

which affect them. Some people are more resistant to change than others. By supplying them with background about decisions, such as factors considered or reasons for a choice, you can help these individuals in their adjustment.

LEADERSHIP DEVELOPMENT

A leader is able to influence followers through the power of authority. This authorization is usually assumed or granted spontaneously by the group, but it always exists. Behavioral scientists inform us that there are three types of leadership authority.

1. *Traditional*—based on the *position* filled by the leader. For example, a choral director working within the jurisdiction of a school has traditional authority as a teacher.
2. *Functional*—based on the leader's *expertise.* This type of authority is stronger because it is related to the leader's competence in his or her field.
3. *Personal*—based on the *personality* and social influence of the leader. This form of authority is best because it promotes a cooperative spirit from the group members.

Obviously, a leader who possesses all three types of authority will have the best potential for motivating people and achieving results. Put in simpler language, this means that an appointed choral director who can combine musical skill with "friendly persuasion" will probably be the most successful.

Achieving Personal Authority

The ability to elicit willing responses from others is largely dependent on one's personality. David Ewen, in discussing the characteristics of a good conductor, contends ". . . a magnetic personality is as important to a conductor as scholarship, and much more essential than either perfect pitch or a photographic memory."[3]

Personality is determined by fairly permanent characteristics, but it can always be improved. Here are some helpful suggestions, guaranteed to help you become a better motivator.

1. Develop *and maintain* a wholesome, cheerful outlook on life, people,

---

[3]David Ewen, *Dictators of the Baton* (Chicago: Ziff-Davis Publishing Company, 1943), p. 9.

and music. Groups respond to enthusiastic leaders. And enthusiasm is generated by optimism. Sometimes rehearsal pressures can cause a certain amount of anxiety or hostility. Too many of these frustrations cause "job tarnish." Three important rules can help minimize negative reactions.

* Do not take things too personally.
* Try to find some sense of humor in all situations.
* Develop an ability to bounce back from unpleasant incidents.

The only way to maintain optimism is by cultivating a positive manner and viewpoint. Positiveness is also the most natural way to gain confidence and to develop self-control for working with people who sing. The ability to see inherent good in self and others will mark the difference between a director who "fills a slot" and a dynamic leader.

2. Develop a penchant for flexibility and vitality. Nothing is more ironic than an eager choral group held back by a deadweight director. The energetic leader is always looking for ways to avoid rehearsal staleness or numbed interpersonal relationships. This interest in group vitality demands concern for his or her own personal health and physical condition.

    To maintain flexibility, you will need to guard against mental ruts. Procrustean thinking, commonly called "putting square pegs in round holes," leads to petrification. There *are* other works suitable for Easter besides Handel's "Hallelujah Chorus," especially when the choir sopranos cannot reach the high A.

3. Cultivate patience and tact. In working with people who sing, always try to be sensitive to the working conditions and moods of your performers. Max Rudolf, in discussing rehearsal techniques, makes the following observation:

    A flair for what to say, and what not to say, is part of a conductor's psychological perception and calls for presence of mind. To know how to word criticisms, to feel when to give encouragement, to sense when a tense moment is best relieved by a joking remark, all this affects the relationship between the leader and his group.[4]

Sometimes problems work themselves out better if treated gently rather than with force. Patient understanding does have its virtue,

---

[4]Max Rudolf, "Rehearsal Techniques," *The Conductor's Art,* ed. Carl Bamberger (New York: McGraw-Hill Book Company, 1965), pp. 290–91.

especially when applied to artistic endeavor. And the director who has not learned to get his or her ego out of the way in uptight situations will be unable to develop that unique quality called graciousness.

4. Be an idealist. In spite of admonitions to be practical by the world's pragmatists, there will always be leaders who, through a desire for something better than life's mediocrity, will bring untold happiness and success to others. The point is, one can be an idealist *and* a realist if ways can be found to transform ideals into attainable goals. Groups are only inspired by leaders with inspiration. And ideals convey a feeling of purpose and a sense of progress.

GROUP DYNAMICS—THE KEY TO SUCCESS

Anyone who follows the progress of baseball or football teams knows that it is possible to have good coaches and talented players but still not be able to come up with a winning team. Organizations must "put it all together" if they are to succeed. The procedure for attaining this coordinated group effort is called group dynamics. According to sociologists, the following three conditions or stages are necessary:

- Stage 1—Organizational Self-motivation
- Stage 2—Organizational Cohesion
- Stage 3—Organizational Morale

Organizational Self-Motivation

Individuals tend to achieve more as members of a group. Groups, in turn, tend to accomplish more when they are allowed to participate in decision making. Scientific studies show that work output, interest, responsibility, originality, and friendliness are greater when a group's leader practices a democratic rather than an authoritarian or *laissez-faire* form of leadership behavior.

Choral directing does not always lend itself well to this type of guidance. In many instances you will have to make arbitrary decisions. But it is because of this situation that you should make a continual effort to consult the ensemble's officers and members whenever possible. During rehearsals try the self-motivation approach by playing the role of a catalyst, releasing energies that already exist in the group. For example, rather than criticizing an ensemble for poor performance, ask the following questions:

- Were you satisfied with your performance?
- Why was the performance inferior?
- What suggestions do you have for improvement?

The responses are often sincere. Sometimes they lead to intense individual involvement and personal commitment. In several instances, I have been requested to schedule extra rehearsals by choral members.

Organizational Cohesion

As individuals begin to feel a sense of belonging, cohesiveness occurs. The relative strength of this togetherness is determined by the attraction the group has for its members. A highly cohesive situation brings about what is commonly known as *esprit de corps*. The result of such a close-knit feeling is coordinated effort and action. According to James Coleman, groups imbued with a sense of teamwork,

> . . . tend to develop characteristic ways of doing things and, concurrently, strong feelings that these are the way things *should* be done—that these are the "normal" ways, the "right" ways.[5]

Cohesion is very important for a singing organization.

- It gives the ensemble a sense of identity.
- It encourages mutual confidence and loyalty between the membership and the director.
- It promotes a stronger cooperative spirit.

Learn to encourage team spirit so that singers can be mobilized toward key group goals. Here are some suggestions:

- Develop standard procedures which are worthy of becoming traditions.
- Encourage the sharing of common values.
- Emphasize the importance of individual responsibility to the group.
- Stimulate individuals through objective demands tied into acknowledged group goals.

---

[5]Coleman, op. cit., p. 278.

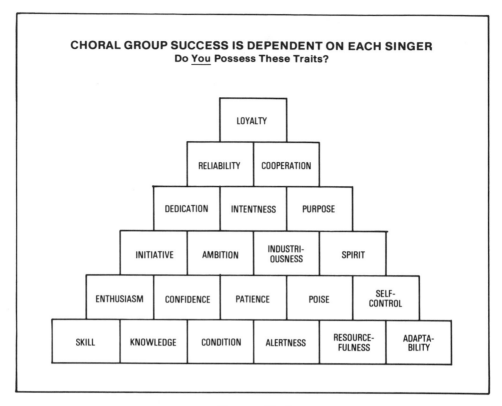

Figure 7–2

Organizational Morale

Morale develops only as a result of cohesion and can best be described as a prevailing mood of confidence in the group's ability to cope with problems. This collective mental condition is achieved when the organization shows a willingness to accept discipline and endure hardship. Only through a strong sense of group spirit can the choral ensemble move toward artistic refinement and musical growth. Standards may be established as a result of cohesiveness, but they will only be met as a result of morale.

Morale is the driving force behind human action. It reaches its ultimate stage when members of the group become convinced that everyone is striving together for something more important than self. You can best instill morale by establishing a competitive spirit among your singers and by providing incentives. For example:

- The ensemble can be challenged to perform better than last year.

- The group can be compared with similar ensembles.
- Individuals can compete for solos.

Sometimes high morale can be encouraged by showing singers how their basic commitments and personal attributes will affect the success of the organization. A very effective way is to provide new members with a Choral Group Success Chart. (See Figure 7–2.)

CHAPTER 8

WORKING WITH SINGERS

Successful choral directors have a "feel" for working with singers. There are, of course, instances where conductors unfamiliar with vocal techniques have managed to pull off polished performances. Usually, however, these successes result from trained or enthusiastic singers and in spite of their leader's limitations.

Therefore, as a choral director you need to become intimately acquainted with the mechanics of singing. There are five specific reasons for this:

- So that you may obtain a wider repertoire of vocal expression from your singers
- So that these responses will be achieved with a minimum of vocal strain
- So that you will use vocal techniques which are compatible with standards of proper singing
- So that you will be aware of individual and ensemble vocal problems
- So that you may communicate better with your singers

ESTABLISHING VOCAL CONCEPTS

Most choral ensembles are comprised of singers with little or no formal training. Through personal experience, I have found they improve faster when they are taught some basic concepts of vocal technique. I usually deal with a new concept at the beginning of each rehearsal until I have completed this orientation. Later, you can build on initial understandings and skills or review what was learned earlier.

Posture

Good singing is achieved through proper breathing; and proper breathing requires correct posture. One way to demonstrate this is to have the ensemble sing a short musical selection while deliberately "crunched" in their seats followed immediately by performance of the same music while standing. The singers should be able to hear considerable improvement in vocal quality during the second rendition. A discussion of ways to achieve correct posture should follow this experience. Here are some important points:

- The chest should be kept comfortably high to free the rib cage for breathing.
- Legs should be straight but not "locked."
- Feet should be shoulder width apart and pointing at an angle of approximately 45 degrees.
- Shoulders should be pulled slightly back, not hunched forward.
- Arms should hang comfortably at the side. If folders are used, they should be held away from the chest to avoid constriction.
- The chin should not be excessively raised or lowered.
- When seated, singers should bend only their knees. The upper torso should remain erect.

Suggested Activities

1. Have your singers stand tall and raise their hands high over their heads. Arms should then be lowered slowly while maintaining a high chest position.

2. Divide your ensemble into two-person teams. Have them spot-correct each other for posture.

Breathing and Support

When ensemble singers run out of breath in the middle of musical phrases, it is usually because they forget to "tank up" with enough air.

I like to begin the introduction of this topic by performing a song such as *America the Beautiful* in one breath to demonstrate how long it is possible to sustain tone. Then, I cover the following points:

- Breathing for singing is a conscious, active, and energized process.
- In order for air to fill the lungs, singers must breath "down and out" so that the rib cage expands.
- The discomfort of wanting to take a breath before reaching the end of a phrase "comes with the territory." Good singers keep singing and thereby develop their capacity to sustain.

Suggested Activities

1. Have singers pretend to suck through a straw for a slow count of five, hold breath for five, then emit a pinpoint "hiss" for fifteen counts. While inhaling, have them place their hands on hips and try to push outward.

2. Have singers lie on their backs with a book on their stomachs. Ask them to observe the rising and falling of the books while breathing. Explain that this is deep (thoraxial) breathing and is preferable to shallow (clavicular) breathing. Have them stand, then sustain and control a long-held tone. As they approach the "discomfort level," point out how they are experiencing healthy muscular antagonism between the diaphragm and the intercostal (rib) muscles.

3. Ask singers to sustain a breathy tone (in the lower part of their range), observing how quickly the air is lost. Then, have them perform a non-breathy tone (in the medium part of their range), while holding back the emission of air to observe how dry and tense the tone becomes. Explain the need to balance emission of air with tone to achieve good quality.

4. Have singers pretend to blow out several candles by puffing. Get them to observe how their diaphragms "kick." Explain how the diaphragm plays a particularly active role in the performance of fast-moving musical passages. Have singers perform an upward- and downward-moving scale at a brisk tempo, using "hah" for each pitch to experience diaphragmatic action.

Phonation

The initial emission of tone should be a coordinated yet spontaneous act, as in speaking. Untrained singers sometimes try to "set up" or overprepare for singing. Results may vary from breathiness to various types of tension.

One approach I find useful is to have singers speak the five principal vowels (*ah, eh, ee, oh, oo*), then "speak" the same vowels on a single, short pitch. A clear, unforced tone should result.

It is also important to get singers into the habit of producing tone with an open throat. "Yawning" the vowel *oh* while singing up and down a five-note scalar passage helps to encourage a "deep-set" position and a mature, natural tone.

Suggested Activities

Tension is often the most detrimental hindrance to proper phonation. The following exercises will help to free up your singers:

1. Have them "buzz" their lips on upward and downward glissandos.

2. Have singers open their mouths, then move their tongues rapidly from side to side.

3. Have them pretend to chew gum to loosen jaws.

Quality

Proper posture, support, and phonation, while important, will not guarantee good tone quality. If the full, natural potential of the voice is left unexplored or undeveloped, singers will tend to perform with a weak or "thin" tone.

In my opinion, the ability to perform a latitude of contrasting choral styles while maintaining a rich tone quality is a hard-earned yet highly desirable goal. I believe if directors would spend more time on this aspect of singing technique, problems such as faulty intonation, poor blend, and lethargic performance would be minimized.

Vowels are the vehicles of tone quality. If they are enunciated correctly and placed properly, there is a good chance the resultant tone will be clear and undistorted. To achieve sonority, an additional task is required. The back of the throat *must* be kept open and the soft palate kept raised. Projection of tone is best achieved by resonation rather than shouting. When tone is allowed to flow unimpeded upward behind the soft palate, resonation will be enhanced, resulting in a "bigger" tone rather than simply a "louder" tone.

Suggested Activities

1. Have singers place their left hand against the side of their face with the little finger positioned near the mouth and the remaining fingers spread one inch apart. Instruct them to sing an *ee* vowel in the front of the mouth near the little finger. The remaining vowels, *eh*, *ah*, *oh*, and *oo*, should be sung on the same pitch and placed in order, from front to rear, at the other finger locations. Later, this exercise should be performed on various pitches so that singers can discover ideal placement of vowel-tones.

2. Singers speak several *uhs* to encourage back open throats. Have them resume the previous exercise while maintaining the open throat position. They should hear a larger, fuller sound.

3. Singers sustain the vowel sound *uh* to maintain an open throat while gradually closing lips. The resultant hum should be tension-free and resonant. Vowels can then be "mixed in" with "*ms*" on various pitches to achieve resonance.

NOTE: Singers sometimes become confused when attempting to sing the front vowels *ee* and *eh* while maintaining an open throat. I find it useful to explain that the tone must go both forward *and* upward at the same time.

Range

Inexperienced singers tend to equate force with the performance of high and low pitches. However, proper production at any pitch level is dependent on coordination between the placement of tone and the amount of breath flow. For example, high pitch requires production of a "light" tone which the singer attempts to place high in the head well above the throat. Support is energized so that an abundance of exhaled air will sustain the tone. On the other hand, low pitch requires production of a "heavier" tone which the singer attempts to place in the chest. Air flow must be minimalized to prevent sharping or tensing the tone.

Suggested Activities

1. Have singers "coo" on relatively high pitch levels to achieve a sense of high head placement. Follow this immediately with a more sustained singing of high pitches on *oo*. Ask singers to envision phonation of each tone as a "pinpoint attack."

2. Singers perform *ah* on a medium high pitch, then begin to gradually add pitches above one whole step at a time, always returning to the low pitch in between. This approach helps them ease into higher notes and gently stretch the voice.

3. Singers learn to "pour" into the low range by singing medium-low pitches on *huh* and glissandoing down the interval of a fifth.

Agility

The ability to perform rapidly changing pitches requires extra mental alertness and especially responsive control of the breathing muscles. The vocal tone should be bright rather than "swallowed" and buoyant rather than weighty. Problems are encountered when singers take too long to produce specific tones or "dwell" too long on a pitch before moving on. Another common problem is the tendency to "gloss over" pitches without achieving sufficient sonority. The key to agility is not simply to move rapidly, but to establish properly produced tones with precision, then move on without collapsing the breath support.

Suggested Activities

1. Singers perform upward and downward moving scalar passages at moderate tempo on syllable *hah*. They place one hand on their abdomen to make sure abdominal muscles are firm during the exercise. Scalar passages are gradually accelerated and the *h* preceding the vowel is eliminated while still maintaining substance of tone.

2. Singers perform an upward and downward moving arpeggio at a moderate tempo. Speed is increased when the ensemble can perform with proper intonation and steady rhythm.

CHOOSING EFFECTIVE WARM-UPS

In Chapter 6, the importance of beginning rehearsals with various types of physical, mental, and vocal exercises was discussed. It is my personal conviction that exercises can make or break an ensemble. Simply put, unless your singers are willing to apply themselves to *productive* vocal exercising, you will probably never reach group potential.

But, let's face it, for many directors warming up the choir seems to be a necessary evil. I must admit, I used to find the routine of mulling through several drills a boring experience. The singers were inevitably restless, and little seemed to be accomplished other than clearing vocal cobwebs. Then, I began to experiment and discovered some important facts.

- A planned variety of exercises made activities more interesting, and vocalists became better motivated.
- When the purpose of a new exercise was briefly explained, singers approached the task as a challenging game.
- The ensemble was just as easily warmed up through exercises which also dealt with specific group vocal problems.

Obviously, these changes have required me to continually expand my repertoire of exercises, often by creating new ones. The results, however, have more than justified my efforts.

Some Facts About Exercises

How do you know if an exercise is a good one? Here are several factors to consider when you are choosing or devising exercises.

1. *Before the voice itself can be "awakened," the body should be readied*

for action. Physical exercises contributing to good posture and active readiness should be included.

2. *Proper singing depends on getting clear signals from the brain.* This in turn requires alertness and concentration. Mental exercises which challenge aural perception and musical response will help your singers get in "the mental swing of things."

3. *Vocal exercises must adhere to fundamentals of proper singing.* Do not expect your tenors to hum pianissimo above a high G. Over a period of time the results would be disastrous. Similarly, one would not choose forte exercises which demand deep chest tones from a young alto section. Good exercises allow the voice to blossom; bad exercises place undue stress on singing technique.

4. *Exercises must be applied clinically.* No one exercise will guarantee results just because it has proven to be successful for others. An exercise is like a prescription—it must be chosen as a remedy for an individual group at a particular time. Ensemble attitude, level of musical development, and vocal growth are some of the factors to be considered. Quite often a new vocal problem replaces an old one. To avoid or ignore these changes by continuing exercises which have lost their effectiveness or usefulness is to run the risk of stagnating your choral program.

5. *Whenever possible, exercises should be taken from actual music.* The primary reason for exercising is to prepare the vocal group for performance. This means that those exercises which come closest to helping singers perform their music better will have the most relevance. Figure 8–1 contains an exercise designed to improve vocal agility. It was derived from those demanding runs found in the *Messiah* chorus, "For Unto Us a Child Is Born." By modulating the drill and stressing proper articulation of each note, the ensemble will have less difficulty when it comes to actually performing Handel's work.

6. *Good exercises accomplish more than one objective.* The exercise period cannot take up an inordinate amount of rehearsal time, and good exercises save time by meeting primary and secondary vocal needs. For example, the exercise in Figure 8–2 is primarily designed to promote resonant sonority, yet it also gives singers the experience of singing whole tones with proper chordal intonation.

Planning Daily Exercises

As a general rule, exercise activities should be considered on a daily basis along with repertoire planning. This does not necessarily mean that new

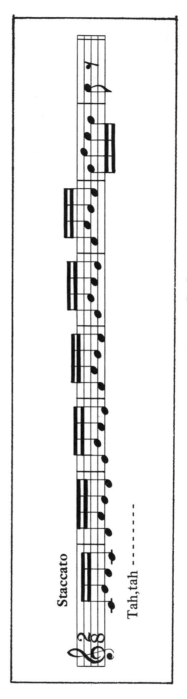

Figure 8–1

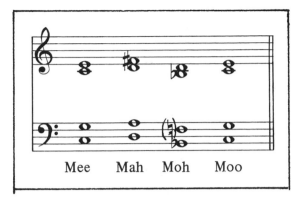

Mee   Mah   Moh   Moo

Figure 8–2

exercises will be chosen every day. Some are designed for long-range improvement, and to eliminate them suddenly might defeat their purpose. On the other hand, exercises which have grown stale or lost their effectiveness need replacing. When you are evaluating each day's activities, ask yourself the following questions:

- What vocal problems need to be corrected?
- What aspects of ensemble singing need improving?
- What performance problems exist within current and upcoming repertoire?
- What areas of general musicianship or mental alertness need attention?

The next step is to change, add, or modify exercises to accomplish your objectives at the next rehearsal.

A Typical Warm-up Procedure

The following exercises could be used at the beginning of a "typical" rehearsal:

1. *Physical Exercises*
   Objective No. 1: Proper posture. Singers pretend they are being pulled up by a rope attached to an imaginary hook in the top of their heads.
   Objective No. 2: Invigoration. Singers turn to the right and rub each others' shoulders. They then turn to the left and repeat the procedure.

Objective No. 3: Body freedom. Singers spread out, place hands on hips, and take a moderately wide stance. They then stretch at the waist by alternately bobbing upper torso to the left and to the right three times.

2. *Mental Exercises*

Objective No. 1: Rhythmic perception. Director claps one measure of rhythm and then continues with new rhythms as ensemble imitates at one measure delay.

Objective No. 2: Melodic perception. Director sings or plays one measure of melody and then continues with new melodic material as ensemble imitates at one measure delay.

Objective No. 3: Musical memorization. Director places short melody on chalkboard. Singers perform and then study the music. Melody is erased, and singers perform from memory.

3. *Vocal Exercises*

Objective No. 1: Initial phonation and gentle opening of chest voice. Singers perform five-note descending scale (see Figure 8–3). A relaxed, open throat is stressed. Begin the exercise in the middle range and move each sequence up by half steps until the beginning note is comfortably high. At this point, reverse the process by moving the sequence downward until the final note is comfortably low.

Objective No. 2: Controlled range extension. Singers perform arpeggiated-scalar exercise. (See Figure 8–4.) Dynamics and articulation require singers to use careful support and placement when they are ascending. Begin exercise in moderately low key and then move upward.

Objective No. 3: Sustained tone singing. Singers perform chorale-type exercises such as Figure 8–5. Director emphasizes supported legato singing at various tempos and dynamic levels.

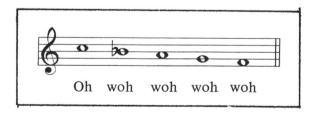

Oh   woh   woh   woh   woh

Figure 8–3

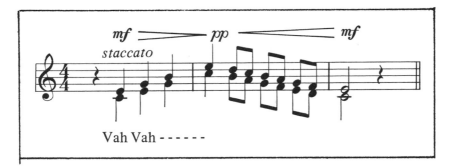

Figure 8–4

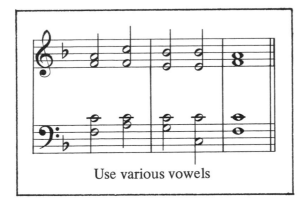

Figure 8–5

DEVELOPING ENSEMBLE SKILLS

The role of the choral director has occasionally been compared to the captain of a ship whose task is to mold the skills and interests of his sailors into a smoothly-functioning crew.

Ensemble Performance Requires Teamwork

All choirs have their share of vocal leaders and followers. This is a natural and desirable thing as long as all work toward a well-balanced, cohesive product. The choral director's role in this regard is that of a catalyst, channeling individual efforts in the group's general direction.

This brings us to a discussion of soloists. In most instances, these individuals are able to make significant contributions without destroying the balance or blend of an ensemble. Occasionally, I have found it necessary to ask those with a healthy vibrato or projection to control their contributions. I also believe that there are instances in which a soloist should not be asked to join a choral organization. An exceptionally powerful and penetrating voice should not be expected to operate at half-speed. This is especially true for smaller chamber ensembles which, ironically, seem to draw the attention of soloists the most.

Sometimes a young singer has vocal problems which dictate special consideration. Just recently I restricted one of my altos to light singing in choir rehearsals because she was having range coordination problems in her voice lessons. After two weeks she regained her vocal balance and was permitted to resume normal singing.

Aside from such individual matters, keep in mind that your primary duty is to stress vocal teamwork. This means that all exercises and directions will be conditioned by consideration for group improvement. In fact, it is my belief that all successful choral directors secretly share the following motto:

Insistence on group vocal teamwork is the key to ensemble success.

Five Key Vocal Areas

Choral ensembles are usually evaluated *vocally* according to the following criteria:

- Intonation
- Attacks and releases
- Blend
- Balance
- Tone

Other aspects such as diction, interpretation, and musicality are also considered and are discussed later in this book. By troubleshooting for inadequacies and providing appropriate exercises, you can improve your ensemble's vocal performance. (See Situation 8–A.) Here are some suggestions.

1. *Intonation*
   a. Common problems. Faulty pitch is usually caused by singers who either do not hear their part contextually or who have a vocal production problem inhibiting them from singing in tune.

SITUATION 8–A

Peter Y. was a master at improving tone quality but rarely worked on listening perception. Consequently, his choral ensembles had a reputation for singing with a hearty, robust sound slightly out of tune!

---

b. *Procedures.* A cappella exercises which require singers to "think with their inner ear" work best. The director must insist on proper vowel formation and adequate support since these two factors are instrumental in maintaining proper intonation.

c. *Suggested exercises*

Objective No. 1: Inner ear development. Singers perform choral work until signalled to cease. They continue to read music silently until signalled to come in again. Repertoire will vary from simple unison melodies to difficult four-part works, depending on the group's level of development.

Objective No. 2: Chordal tuning. Singers begin chord. (See Figure 8–6.) Each section moves up by half step until entire chord has been modulated upward. Flow of continued sound is maintained by using staggered breathing.

Objective No. 3: Interval recognition. Singers perform intervals in unison, as requested by the director. More advanced ensembles

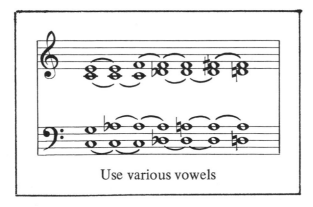

Use various vowels

Figure 8–6

begin on a unison note; however, individual sections move to intervals when requested. These intervals may be prearranged by the director so as to maintain tonality. The use of seconds, tritones, and so on produce an atonal result.

2. *Attacks and releases*

   a. *Common problems.* Ensemble does not sense point at which it should come in or cut off. Sometimes singers are partially impeded from coordinated attacks and releases by consonants, range, and dynamic levels.

   b. *Procedures.* Simple chordal exercises allow singers to concentrate on attacks and releases while the director varies musical conditions.

   c. *Suggested exercises*

   Objective No. 1: Pinpoint entries and releases. Singers perform the word "toot" on single chord. Director varies tempo and dynamic levels. Emphasis on precise initial and final "t" is stressed.

   Objective No. 2: Proper treatment of consonants. Singers perform various consonants and vowels on single chord. Director emphasizes rule of thumb that initial consonants *precede* point of entry cued by the conductor and final consonants are affected at point of release. Tempo, range, and dynamics are varied by the director.

   Objective No. 3: Timely entries after rests. Singers perform repertoire containing lengthy rests for each choral part. The director does not cue entries but insists on accurate attacks by clapping the meter.

3. *Blend*

   a. *Common problems.* Poor blend is sometimes caused by singers with excessive vibrato or shrillness of tone. Most instances, however, result simply because individuals lack ensemble awareness.

   b. *Procedures.* Exercises which help to equalize voices by providing a common denominator work best. For example, concentrating on a single vowel and stressing uniformity of sound will allow individuals to become more sensitized in their ensemble relationship.

   c. *Suggested exercises*

   Objective No. 1: Uniform volume. Simple, four-part exercises are performed on single vowels molto legato. Controlled pianissimo singing is stressed at first. Singers are continually reminded that they must be able to hear their neighbors or they are singing too loud. Eventually, higher dynamic levels are introduced but with emphasis on control.

Objective No. 2: Covered vowels. Simple chorales are used. Begin with humming and then ask singers to *gradually* move into a specific vowel without changing the quality of the tone. At first, use "back" vowels (*oh, oo*); later, allow singers to move into "forward" vowels (*ah, eh, ee*). To ensure continuity between the hum and vowels, have singers change back and forth within the chorale.

4. *Balance*
   a. *Common problems.* Ensemble sections are unequal in terms of dynamic weight. This lack of balance tends to be most noticeable at climactic passages.
   b. *Procedures.* Balance problems are best eliminated by seating singers in quartets or repositioning sections so that individuals will begin to sense the relationship of their parts to others. Contrapuntal exercises are good for emphasizing equal loudness between sections when they are stating the subject and lesser volume when they are performing subordinate material.
   c. *Suggested exercises*
      Objective No. 1: Sectional awareness. While singers perform a chorale, the director continually experiments with balances by requesting one section to increase volume, another section to decrease volume, etc.
      Objective No. 2: Dynamic equality. Individual sections perform isolated notes at specific dynamic levels back and forth to each other. The singers note their "differences of opinion" and then, guided by the director, learn to match volume at each dynamic level.

5. *Tone*
   a. *Common problems.* Singers have difficulty producing and maintaining an even sonority and richness of tone, especially when they are performing soft or low pitches.
   b. *Procedures.* Initial exercising should facilitate the development of intensity as a norm of singing. Later exercises should require singers to maintain this quality of singing under more demanding musical conditions.
   c. *Suggested exercises*
      Objective No. 1: *Resonant sonority.* Singers emphasize consonant *m* in following exercise. (See Figure 8–7.) Modulate up by half steps.
      Objective No. 2: Singing softly with intensity. Simple chordal exercises and chorales are performed at forte, mezzo forte, piano,

and pianissimo dynamic levels consecutively. The director demands *increased* support for each repetition.

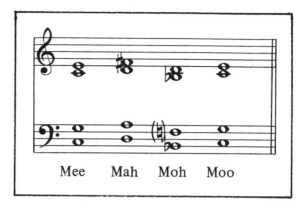

Figure 8–7

SECTIONS AND INDIVIDUALS

For the most part, it is possible to deal collectively with all singers in an ensemble and get good vocal results by using generalized techniques. For example, all choir members will benefit equally from breathing exercises, regardless of voice type. Sooner or later, however, you will be required to solve a problem for an individual section of voices. (See Situation 8–B.)

SITUATION 8–B

James M. directed a male glee club for years until the private school became coeducational. He had difficulty getting a good sound from his new soprano and alto sections. After visiting and observing rehearsals at a nearby girl's academy, Jim found ways to improve his trebles.

The Soprano Voice

1. *Range* (optimum range for more mature voices given in brackets)

Figure 8–8

2. *Tessitura*

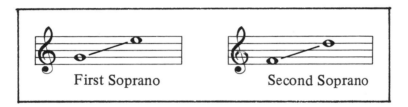

Figure 8–9

3. *Ideal qualities:* Flutelike sound; buoyancy and agility
4. *Undesirable tendencies:* Shrillness; thinness of tone; breathiness

The Alto Voice

1. *Range*

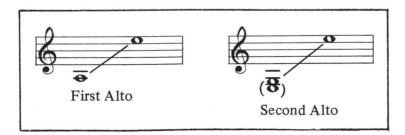

Figure 8–10

2. *Tessitura*

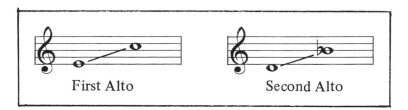

Figure 8–11

3. *Ideal qualities:* Round, full-bodied sound; mellowness
4. *Undesirable tendencies:* Hootiness; wobble

The Tenor Voice

1. *Range*

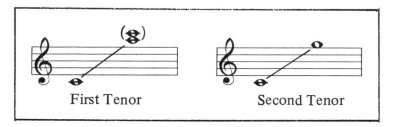

Figure 8–12

2. *Tessitura*

Figure 8–13

3. *Ideal qualities;* Lyricism; head voice
4. *Undesirable tendencies:* Blatant, pushed-up high notes; pinched sound

The Bass Voice

1. *Range*

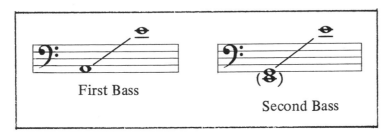

Figure 8–14

2. *Tessitura*

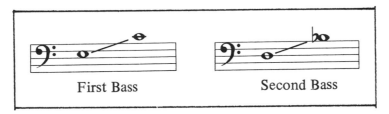

Figure 8–15

3. *Ideal qualities:* Resonant supporting tones; exactness of pitch
4. *Undesirable tendencies:* Boominess; unwieldy sounds

The "In-Between Voice": How to Make the Best of It

Occasionally you will find singers whose compass of singable notes falls smack in between two choral parts. This situation usually occurs with mezzo-sopranos and baritones of limited range. These individuals should not be avoided because they cannot be pigeonholed into a preconceived vocal category. Quite often, they may be utilized effectively as what I call "swivel chairs." For example, a young baritone who cannot reach lower notes may be assigned to the bass section with the following instructions:

- Sing low notes beyond your reach up an octave.
- Sing the tenor part in places where additional support is needed.
- Always sing the upper line in divisi bass scoring.

Sometimes one comes across fortunate vocalists who can reach all of the notes in two or more vocal parts. Where should they be placed? The answer is simple: where they will be most comfortable. During the initial audition, time should be spent with these singers to determine exactly where their tessitura lies. This will be the deciding factor.

VOCAL HYGIENE

Some choral directors take what I call a "passive attitude" toward their singers' vocal health. That is, they provide no guidance or precautions regarding vocal hygiene. Then, when their performers become ill or vocally indisposed, they blame these circumstances on bad luck. It is certainly true that little can be done when a flu epidemic hits an entire school. Nevertheless, there are specific steps a choral director should take to minimize vocal casualties.

The following three approaches have proven particularly effective:

- Provide singers with a health checklist.
- Watch for faulty singing.
- Work around vocal ailments.

Provide Singers with a Health Checklist

The best way to avoid poor health or ailments is by establishing a preventative maintenance program. Younger singers are sometimes willing to take chances by running around in cold weather without a coat, shouting at December football games, and so on. If you can get the point across that healthy singers are essential to a good choral ensemble, then you might be able to establish a foothold in preventing unnecessary vocal and health disorders. One effective way to accomplish this is by providing each vocalist with a "Health Checklist." This short list of items can be taped into choir folders and will serve as a constant reminder to keep fit. (See Figure 8–16.)

HEALTH CHECKLIST

- Get enough sleep
- Eat properly
- Dress adequately
- Avoid shouting
- Keep neck covered in cold weather

- Avoid cold liquids before and during singing
- Stay dry in wet weather
- Do not sing with sore throat

Figure 8–16

Watch for Faulty Singing

Some of my fondest memories go back to my early days as a member of a college fraternity. Inevitably, there was the late Saturday night songfest. I will never forget those red faces—and the Sunday morning sore throats which everyone seemed to complain about. Those carefree days at least taught me a lesson about singing, and I try to make sure that my singers do not fall into the same trap. Here are some warning signs of improper vocal production.

- Poor posture, especially a sagging chest
- Tight jaw
- Closed throat
- Tense tongue

The astute choral director will "nip the problem in the bud" through effective remedies. To improve sitting posture, ask your singers to stand and then sit on the edge of their seats without changing the erectness of their upper torsos. Tenseness and tightness can be eliminated by introducing loosening-up exercises. Sometimes singers tend to pinch their vowels in a particular musical work. In this case, continual encouragement to keep the vowels open will help to offset improper singing.

Work Around Vocal Ailments

Many a singer has lost an inordinate amount of rehearsal and performance time because one of the following situations occurred:

- The singer was overenthusiastic and tried to sing in spite of a severe vocal disorder.
- The conductor was oblivious to the singer's problem or failed to insist on sufficient recuperation time.

Choral directors are not doctors, but there are steps we should take whenever a "battlefield casualty" occurs.

- Recognize the symptoms and nature of the ailment.
- Be prepared to make an objective decision regarding the indisposed singer's immediate relationship with the ensemble.

For minor vocal inconveniences this may mean asking the member to sing lightly. Those hampered by more severe disorders might attend rehearsals to learn their music but refrain from singing. Severe cases obviously would require complete absence from rehearsals. The common vocal ailments are listed below in order of their severity.

1. *Hoarseness.* Partial loss of the voice accompanied by irritation. Usually the full voice returns again by the next day. Hoarseness occurs most frequently at the beginning of the singing year. First signs are wheezing cough and weeping eyes. At the outset, the singers should take a break and then sing softly upon return. If hoarseness persists, the individual should be given the entire rehearsal off.

2. *Common cold.* Viral attack on the respiratory system, resulting in runny nose and sneezing. Statistics show that as many as 90 percent of your singers will catch a cold during the year, and over half of them will probably have several colds. "Three days coming, three days with you, and three days going" is an old but fairly accurate description of a typical cold cycle.

   Unfortunately, the cold virus is highly communicable, and a hyperactive sneezer can contaminate an entire vocal section. As a general rule, try to give the more "advanced" cases time off, especially when concerts are not impending.

   Vocalists with a cold can usually perform if they have to by "singing over" their imposition. This is achieved as follows:
   - By relying on proper vocal coordination and not pushing their voices.
   - By experimenting with vocal sounds until they obtain maximum clarity for their condition. A relaxed open throat will help in this regard.

3. *Common sore throat.* Inflammation of the pharynx. Often these are mild, transient irritations occurring in conjunction with a cold or as a result of catching a draft. Sore throats also serve as warnings for more serious ailments, particularly strep throat. Singers who complain

should be closely watched and, preferably, should not sing. In some instances, this precaution will save them from coming down with one of the next two incapacitating ailments.

4. *Pharyngitis.* Severe inflammation of the pharynx. Symptoms are significant pain in the throat causing difficulty in swallowing. Phlegm is often present. Under no circumstances should a singer perform with these symptoms. Pharyngitis usually lasts up to seven days.

5. *Laryngitis.* Inflammation of the larynx. This is the most severe of all vocal disorders. Complete loss of the voice for several days is common, but be prepared to lose your ensemble member for as long as two weeks. Progress in regaining the singing voice is slow. If speaking and singing are not approached gradually, a relapse may occur.

In addition to the vocal ailments described, singers suffer from other indispositions which limit their performing ability. Be especially on the lookout for the following problems:

- Respiratory allergies
- Swollen glands
- Toothaches
- Tonsillitis

Whenever any of your choral members run into vocal ailments, it is always a good idea to "touch base" with their voice teachers if they study privately. Individuals with severe problems will benefit by your persuasion to see an ear, nose, and throat specialist.

CHAPTER 9

DEVELOPING
AUTHENTIC
STYLE

One of the primary functions of a conductor is to interpret musical works with appropriate style. Sometimes, the music itself provides clues to its distinctive manner of expression. More often, the choral director's knowledge and understanding of performance practice leads to stylistic accuracy. (See Situation 9–A.)

SITUATION 9–A

Robert P's choruses could perform Bruckner motets with thundering excitement. Unfortunately, his ensembles attempted to perform Bach cantatas and Morley madrigals the same way.

This discussion about stylistic interpretation can best be clarified by answering four essential questions.

1. *Why attempt to achieve stylistic accuracy?* The most obvious answer is: to avoid boredom. When I read music critics' reviews of choral concerts, I frequently find statements to the effect that everything sounded the same. Choral performances are sometimes bland not because of poor programming but because of insufficient stylistic interpretation.

There is, however, another more important reason for performing repertoire with stylistic distinction: music comes to life only when its essence is revealed. You may somehow pull off a performance with technical proficiency and impressive talent, but you will only bring a work to life by fulfilling its stylistic requirements.

2. *What are the problems encountered when you are attempting to achieve stylistic accuracy?* Most difficulties of choral music before the Romantic period are related to its accompaniment. Few ensembles have ready access to authentic instruments used in early period performances. This usually means that a compromise must be made by employing modern instruments and encouraging methods of playing which will bring out as

much as possible of the music's early flavor. For example, string players must be shown how to bow and embellish Baroque works.

On the other hand, harpsichords and recorders are sometimes available, and a little extra effort by the director to locate and use these instruments will go far toward providing a more realistic performance. Not to be overlooked are commonly available percussion instruments which are similar in sound to those used in Renaissance presentations. It is surprising how much vitality can be brought to the interpretation of a sprightly Spanish *villancico* by simply adding a tambourine or snareless drum.

Recently I had the opportunity to hear two contrasting interpretations of Giovanni Gabrieli's polychoral motet *Jubilate Deo*. The first presentation employed organ accompaniment with the double choir. The second performance, however, doubled the voices with two choirs of brass instruments and used the organ accompaniment more judiciously to reinforce climactic sections. This interpretation was an exhilarating one, primarily because the motet received proper stylistic attention.

3. *How can stylistic accuracy best be achieved?* Correct interpretation begins with the director's concept of style. This means that you must learn to recognize styles not only by but also within each period. For instance, Vaughan-Williams and Ligeti are twentieth century choral composers; yet the stylistic requirements of their music differ sharply. Often differences between national styles and even genres must be taken into account.

After the director knows what he or she wants, methods must be found to communicate this information to the performers. Singers need to hear a demonstration of Renaissance vocal tone. Through trial and error various concepts and descriptive ideas are conveyed until the ensemble begins to work successfully toward desired interpretation. Often one word may have an impact on the group and become a trigger for correct stylistic response. I once had difficulty with my choir's interpretation of a Bach cantata until I described the fugue they were performing as "sewing machine music" and asked them to "chatter" as they sang. My imagery hit home, and their interpretation snapped into focus.

Some directors prefer to deal exclusively with technical instructions when they are working with singers. This will not always work when you are trying to achieve stylistic accuracy. For example, you may rightly ask for minimal vibrato in a Gesualdo chromatic madrigal, but it will be the ensemble's *concept* of overall mood and tonal quality which will determine the final interpretive outcome of the work.

4. *Won't changes in vocal interpretation ruin my ensemble's tone quality?* This attitude is ill-founded, because it presumes that a choral group

should have a preconceived sound. Every quality choir I ever heard had *control*, which is completely different from the "one-sound approach." And, more important, each was able to adapt to the music's stylistic demands rather than subjecting a large portion of choral repertoire to the meat-grinder treatment.

When considering stylistic tradition, it is important to remember that exceptions to the rule exist within all chronological periods. For example, during the Baroque period, composers such as Purcell continued to write music in the earlier Renaissance style.

MUSIC TO 1600

The Medieval and Renaissance eras represent an extensive period of at least eleven hundred years. In spite of various stylistic trends, however, there are several musical characteristics which permeate most music from this early period.

- Melodic and linear movement of lines takes precedence over harmonic considerations.

- Modality, rather than tonality, provides characteristic color of all genres until at least 1500.

- Rhythm is often nonmetrical and unstressed.

This extensive period also includes a notable achievement in music history. Gregorian chant and other single line vocal music gave ground to the composition of sacred and secular multi-part works. Because of different stylistic demands, each category is presented separately.

Gregorian Chant

Also known as plainsong, this monophonic vocal music was originally conceived for musical enhancement of early Christian Church Offices and Masses. Chant is restrained and relatively unemotional so as not to interfere with the dignified nature of these services. Melodic movement is primarily step-wise; disjunctive skips and leaps are conservative. Rhythm is free flowing and largely determined by the text and its treatment. For example, "Alleluias" are melismatic (many notes to one syllable), whereas the many-worded "Glorias" and "Credos" are predominantly syllabic (one note per syllable).

1. *Performers.* Gregorian chant is unison music primarily for men's voices. Convents, however, were established as early as the fifth

century where nuns participated in chanting. During the Renaissance period male choirs, consisting of boys and men, performed this vocal music in octaves. My personal preference is to use either males *or* females for Gregorian chant performances. This practice tends to convey a more appealing, authentic interpretation to present-day concert audiences.

Organs were installed in churches as early as the Middle Ages, but they were probably used more for the accompaniment of congregational hymns than for chants. The size of the choir varied from a half dozen singers in a small country church to a large contingent of monks at a monastery. Generally speaking, chanting is best performed by a small to moderate sized choral group.

The director should not fall into the trap of performing all chants with full forces. Psalms require responsorial treatment. This means that a soloist should alternate with the ensemble. Certain sections of the Mass, such as the Introit, Offertory, and Communion, require alternation between two choirs, in antiphonal style. Modern chant book and choral editions often provide directions in this regard. Catholic clergy are usually willing to provide additional help.

2. *Stylistic requirements.* Chanting still exists as an integral activity of the Catholic Church service. But in many instances its practice has been modernized by English translation, organ accompaniment, and so on. When chant is sung in Latin, local and regional versions of pronunciation often prevail. The director should choose a widely accepted pronunciation guide and require singers to follow its rules. I prefer *Pronunciation of Church Latin*, a brochure printed by the American Guild of Organists, 815 Second Avenue, Suite 318, New York, New York 10017.

- *Tonal color.* Purity of tone with little or no vibrato was the objective sought by early singers. This essential character of chant will be attained as your singers learn to hit each pitch "dead center" without slurring. An emphasis on vowels, and a slight de-emphasis on such aspirated consonants as *t* and *k*, will also help to preserve chant's legato nature. A cappella unison singing is difficult and requires special attention to intonation. One faulty voice may pull the entire ensemble off pitch. Proper blending is also important, for vocalists who stick out will tend to destroy rhythmic coordination.
- *Phrasing.* Singers must be trained to spin out phrases without taking obtrusive breaths in the middle of lines. When phrases of

extended length are encountered, carefully rehearsed staggered breathing may be necessary. Chanting several syllables or words to individual tones also requires special coordination. These types of chants are frequently encountered in Renaissance Magnificats where Gregorian chant verses are interspersed with multi-part choral sections. In some instances, choosing a soloist for the chant sections may save considerable rehearsal time.

- *Dynamics.* Crescendos and decrescendos should be scrupulously avoided. Such practice was branded "self-display" and condemned by church clergy. Be especially careful not to place a diminuendo on final notes.
- *Tempo.* The overall speed of a particular chant should be determined by its text. Solemn words require slower tempos; psalms of praise are more vigorous. Early period singers became adept at slowing the ends of phrases, and the director should attempt to capture this ebb and flow, which is so essential to chanting.

3. *Improvisation.* Chants are constructed out of various modes which usually avoid leading tones. Early period singers, however, added sharps to certain notes so as to create a feeling of finality at cadences (other tones were flattened to avoid the tritone). This practice was called *musica ficta.* The problem with such alteration is that it tends to destroy Gregorian chant's modal character. For this reason I feel that *musica ficta* should be avoided when you are performing plainsong.

4. *Conducting problems.* The early practice of conducting chant with the use of suggestive pitch signs was called *chironomy.* Because plainsong is based on free-verse rhythm, today's metrical patterns for conducting are really not geared to such music. Once a particular Gregorian chant has been chosen for performance, experiment with various circular and linear arm movements until motions are found which best express the character of each musical phrase.

Sacred Polyphonic Music

Early sacred multi-part music owes much of its character to preestablished Gregorian chant. It, too, is restrained and austere when compared with secular music of the same period. More important, plainsong is usually employed as a foundation (*cantus firmus*) within these religious works, where it quite often appears in the tenor vocal line.

The original chant is frequently separated into shorter parts by the composer so that each segment may be used to establish a different musical section. These sections are, in turn, overlapped, resulting in a continuous outpouring of sound permeated by interwoven strands of lines. Occasional contrasts are obtained through the use of less active homophonic (chordal) sections. Motets, Masses, and Magnificats comprise the bulk of early sacred polyphonic repertoire.

1. *Performers.* Church choirs varied in size from half a dozen to approximately eighteen singers. The Sistine Chapel in Rome maintained an unusually large choir of thirty performers during the Renaissance period. Obviously, presenting this type of music with a chorus of one hundred singers would be unacceptable.

   Contrary to popular belief, a cappella singing was but one of several ways to perform an early sacred composition. Sometimes the church's organ was used to softly accompany singers. Instruments, such as the fidel (early stringed instrument), the recorder, and the crumhorn (early oboe), often doubled the vocal lines in performance.

   Choral directors should experiment with combinations of available instruments and voices. Figure 9–1 presents a typical solution for achieving a more authentic sound. By employing various modes of performance, you can achieve significant contrasts. This is especially important when you are presenting several Medieval or Renaissance works within the same program.

DISTRIBUTION OF INSTRUMENTS FOR EARLY PERIOD SACRED MUSIC PERFORMANCE

Vocal Part	Doubling Instrument
Soprano	Recorder (Flute)
Alto	Viola
Tenor	Oboe
Bass	Violoncello

Figure 9–1

---

2. *Stylistic requirements*
   - *Tonal color.* As with Gregorian chant, vibrato was minimal or nonexistent *between* vocal sections. However, it is important to tune intervals at all times. A lighter, relatively thin tone quality is

also desirable. Tenors should rely more on falsetto for high notes, and basses should make frequent use of head voice.

- *Phrasing.* Because choirsters sang from part books, they became adept at observing melodic direction, spinning out phrases, and stressing important words. Contemporary directors need to spend time training their singers to think horizontally rather than vertically. The Bach chorale approach will not work for most Renaissance sacred polyphony. One solution is to have singers read the text aloud to the rhythm of their part so that they may achieve a sense for rises and falls within their vocal line.

- *Dynamics.* Although directions for loudness and softness were not written in the part books, dynamics were undoubtedly used in conjunction with the rise and fall of melodic lines. Certainly, textual acclamations such as "*Et resurrexit . . .*" called for more of a forte sound than "*Et incarnatus est . . .*" Openings of points of imitation need to be brought out slightly while other parts recede. And suspended notes require a slight emphasis before they resolve. Early period sacred music, however, is reserved music, and choral directors should be both conservative and discrete in their employment of dynamics.

- *Tempo.* Renaissance music was universally regulated by a relatively fixed duration of time called the *tactus* (beat). According to scholars, this uniform speed was closely related to pulse rate and is comparable to our present day slow or moderately slow tempo. Composers achieved changes in speed by changing notational values withing the composition. Thus, the conductor's duty was to establish and maintain a uniform beat, allowing the music to unfold with its built-in changes of pace naturally taking place. There was, however, a tendency to gather forces together on the penultimate tone before settling on the final note. During syllabic (one note per word) sections, tempo was slightly increased.

3. *Improvisation.* Although *musica ficta* was employed by singers, the question of when and how often to alter notes has been a perplexing one for musicologists. Introducing leading tones will make cadences more forceful, but it will also orient modal compositions more towards major or minor tonality. Modern reliable editions of Medieval and Renaissance choral music identify places where the rules of *musica ficta* may be applied by placing a sharp or flat above the pertinent note. Ultimately, however, you as the director must decide. Play through a composition using both approaches. You may choose either

the plain or the altered version. When you are combining the two, be careful not to introduce inconsistencies between vocal lines.

4. *Conducting problems.* Although modern editions usually employ bar lines, downbeat stress must be minimized. One of the conductor's prime responsibilities is to maintain a steady, unaccented tempo. As a matter of fact, it would be better to establish an even series of hand or finger movements rather than forcing the ensemble to contend with an erratic conducting pattern. The left hand is especially useful for helping present-day singers with their melodic interpretation by molding and shaping individual lines at strategic places.

Secular Polyphonic Music

Early period secular choral repertoire tends to fall into two categories.

- Classic madrigals, similar in format to the religious motets. These are stylistically mannered and often depend on chromaticism for word painting and coloristic effects. Even when they are plaintive, they are more passionate than their sacred counterparts.

- Lighter Italian canzonettas, English ballads, Spanish villancicos, and so on. These are strophic works, often containing homophonic refrains in triple meter. Many are written with conciseness and tend toward a hearty, robust character.

1. *Performers.* Secular vocal music was primarily intended for private performance by small groups. Even when it was performed for the public, only one or two singers usually sang each part. The intimate nature of these works should be preserved by presenting them with chamber-sized ensembles. Many pieces are ideal for solo groups such as trios and quartets.

   As with sacred choral music of the same period, instruments often doubled the vocal parts. Another prevalent practice was the substitution of instruments for voices. For example, if a bass singer was unavailable for a music-making session, a lira da gamba (early violoncello) might have been played instead. Quite often a vocal work was performed as a solo by having the top line sung while several instruments performed the bottom parts. Many late sixteenth century English ayres were provided in two versions by the composer. One arrangement required a vocal soloist accompanied by lute; the other version employed only singers.

2. *Stylistic requirements*
   - *Tonal color.* Pureness of tone and clarity of line are essential as with all early period vocal forms. More variety of color is necessary, however, than for sacred music. Composers such as Jannequin even require imitations of birds and street cries. Basses need to be nimble so that they can keep up with others in their handling of thematic material.
   - *Phrasing.* Contrapuntal sections usually consist of overlapping phrases. These require catch breaths and staggered breathing so as not to interrupt momentum. Homophonic sections require coordinated ensemble breathing. In lighter, dance-like works, the rhythmic interplay between vocal parts should be emphasized.
   - *Dynamics.* Secular works sometimes contain repeated sections which should be performed at contrasting dynamic levels. The first statement is often sung forte; the repeat is performed piano. This process may be reversed at the end of a work to gain a more climactic effect. As with early sacred music, dynamics may be conservatively employed in conjunction with the natural rise and fall of phrases. Slight crescendos on long-held notes, especially suspensions, can be effective when they are carefully controlled.
   - *Tempo.* Be on the alert for modern editions containing an overabundance of half and whole notes. Unless the work is a lamentation or a melancholic love song, this probably means that the scholar who transcribed the music from its original manuscript failed to bring the notation into line with present-day practice. Let the textual content and the overall mood of the music be a guide to your choice of tempo.

3. *Improvisation.* Besides employing the rules of *musica ficta*, singers were adept at bringing out pertinent words for dramatic effect. One should keep in mind that love songs were often composed and performed with feigned emotion. Words such as "swooning," "weeping," and "dying" should be slightly exaggerated. Dissonant, chromatically altered notes may also be leaned on to achieve their full effect.

4. *Conducting problems.* The relationship between duple and triple meter is important in early period secular music since it occurs so often within many compositions. The correct way to control these transitions is by treating the half note as a common denominator. (See Figure 9–2.)

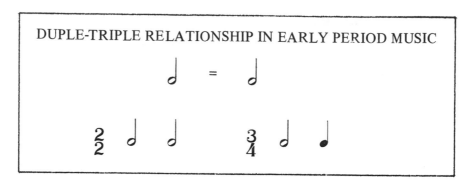

Figure 9–2

THE BAROQUE ERA

Unlike those of the previous period, most genres of the Baroque era were performed with similar stylistic treatment. The primary exceptions were sacred motets occasionally written and performed in the older Renaissance fashion. But for the most part Baroque music, whether it was courtly or religious, was greatly unified in style by the harmonically conceived basso continuo.

Melodic lines became polarized from other parts and took on a more diversified independence ranging from declamatory recitatives to lyrical arias. Modality gave way completely to tonality, and such compositional devices as modulation and functional harmony came into practice. As the period moved into maturity, two basic modes of choral treatment became prevalent and were often used interchangeably within compositions:

- Contrapuntal sections and movements, usually employing extensive runs and perpetual motion.

- Homophonic sections and movements. The chorale exemplifies this type of writing.

1. *Performers.* Large performing groups were the exception rather than the rule. Many of J. S. Bach's cantatas were performed by approximately twelve singers and twenty instrumentalists. Vocal soloists came from within the choir. Instruments commonly used were recorders, viols (early stringed instruments), oboi d'amore (early oboes pitched a minor third lower), bassoons, clarin trumpets, and timpani.

   An adventurous university *collegium musicum* or other such ensemble may be able to present performances using some of these authentic instruments. Directors should at least make an attempt to locate recorder players. Trumpet players who specialize in performing high notes on a modern "Bach trumpet" are sometimes available. Finding viol players is more difficult. One solution is to use gut on regular string instruments to achieve a more mellow and less penetrating sound similar to that of the earlier viols.

Instruments were often substituted for one another, depending on which players were available for performance. You should feel free to use recorders (or flutes) in place of strings and vice versa. Often a practical solution is to combine them on a particular part.

The most important thing to remember in this discussion is the fact that very little a cappella singing actually occurred. Instruments doubled vocal parts in choral works unless they had their own accompanying material to perform. Modern editions of Baroque choral music often overlook this point and fail to provide necessary instrumental parts for so-called a cappella movements. This means, for example, that J.S. Bach's motets should be performed with instruments, and their parts are to be derived from the vocal lines.

The harpsichord was the basic keyboard instrument for secular music; the organ was played in sacred performances. Reversing this procedure, or combining both instruments within the same work, was highly unusual and should be avoided. The keyboard played at all times within a composition, unless a specific section was marked "tacet" by the composer. To help solidify harmonic support, at least one bass instrument always played along with the keyboard. Violoncellos, double basses, and bassoons should be used for this function in present-day performances.

2. *Stylistic requirements*
   - *Tonal color.* Vocal agility was necessary to perform rapid, florid runs. Even in more slowly moving passages, thick, vibrato-ridden singing was avoided. Therefore, tone quality should be clear and relatively thin. Under no circumstances should Baroque choral music be performed using modern-day operatic force.
   - *Phrasing.* Because so much of this period's music employs the principle of perpetual motion, phrases are often extensive and closely juxtaposed with minimal time for pause in between. Maintaining momentum has top priority in these situations, and choristers must learn to skillfully employ catch breaths and staggered breathing.
   - *Dynamics.* Common practice was to employ either forte or piano

volume and reserve other levels of dynamics for special effects. Hence, the term "terraced dynamics" has become a popular term for describing Baroque dynamics. Repetitions of phrases, especially at the end of sections and movements, were frequently performed as echoes. Dissonances were intended as expressive devices and should be performed more loudly than surrounding musical material.

- *Tempo.* Although much of this period's music is fast moving, tempos were controlled and never rushed. Terms such as allegro or largo specified the character of a work rather than a precise speed. Accelerandos and ritardandos did not normally occur within musical phrases.

However, rallentandos were often observed at the end of movements. Their magnitude should be determined by the character of the music. For example, a majestic mood would require a slower broadening.

3. *Improvisation.* Music of this period literally glittered with ornaments added to music in performance. Choral ensembles, however, were expected to perform their parts with minimal embellishment so as not to cloud their parts excessively. As a general rule, restrict choristers to trills at suitable cadences and only when they are singing the melodic line.

Vocal soloists, however, were a different matter. They were expected to ornament their music, especially when performing the repeat sections of da capo (ABA) arias. Nowadays the extent of embellishing will depend on the vocal agility of the singer chosen for performance. Coloratura sopranos are obviously capable of performing more of these flourishes than deep basses. Instrumental ensembles likewise should be encouraged and guided in their performance of ornamentation. This is especially true for instrumentalists who perform solo melodies and obbligatos.

Knowing how and when to embellish Baroque music is not always an easy task. Some choral scores designate basic locations with appropriate signs; others are remiss in this aspect. One initial aid is to listen to recordings of authentic choral performances by such groups as Nikolaus Harnoncourt's Concentus Musicus (recorded on the Telefunken label), observing places in the score where embellishments occur. Consult Thurston Dart's *The Interpretation of Music* for details regarding types of ornaments and their signs.

Baroque music was also performed with stylized crispness. Dotted rhythms were normally executed as though they were double-dotted unless they occurred in conjunction with triplets. (See Figure 9–3.) If you decide to use a relatively large choral ensemble, extra time must be devoted to cleaning up rhythmic articulation as well as attacks and releases.

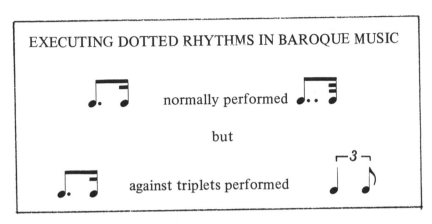

Figure 9–3

THE CLASSICAL PERIOD

One of the outstanding characteristics of Classical period music in general is its emphasis on melodic lyricism. As a result, many melodies achieve a refined and pleasantly ingratiating quality. Harmony, often confined to an accompanistic role, is usually controlled by cleanness of progression and stylistic discreteness. Although contrapuntal writing was carried over from the Baroque era, it became more harmonically saturated. Another salient feature of Classical period music is the symmetrical structure of phrases and the clean delineation of sections within movements

This is also the age of the newly conceived symphony, and its idiomatic characteristics permeate all other forms, including choral music. For example, much of the choral writing in F. J. Haydn's Masses is absorbed into a pervasive symphonic texture. Composers of this period were also affected by the *Sturm und Drang* (Storm and Stress) literary movement. As a result, some choral works contain an abundance of dramatic tension, particularly in developmental and climactic sections. Compositional devices used to achieve this effect include unexpected dynamic changes from piano to forte and sudden crescendos or sforzatos. Yet this display of musical force is inevitably controlled by Classical period unity and form.

1. *Performers.* Performing groups were moderate in size compared to today's standards. Even the very large Salzburg Cathedral, which was musically better equipped than most institutions, limited its performers to the following numbers:
   - Eight to ten vocal soloists
   - Forty to forty-five choral singers
   - Twenty-five to thirty instrumentalists

   During the Classical period, the harpsichord was gradually replaced by the piano over a twenty-year period beginning about 1770. As a general rule, secular choral works composed after 1770 should use piano when keyboard accompaniment is required. Organ was, of course, still used as the accompanying keyboard instrument for sacred music.

2. *Stylistic requirements*
   - *Tonal color.* Lightness and clarity of tone are essential for achieving Classic period elegance of style. Therefore, vibrato should be minimized and lyrical buoyancy maximized in vocal production. Directors, however, should not confuse this with timidity, for a degree of assertiveness is necessary to maintain the rhythmic vitality usually found in this music.
   - *Phrasing.* Musical phrases are often two or four measures in length and paired. Whenever symmetrical structure occurs, performers may be encouraged to perform a slight decrescendo at mid-cadence, followed by light stress at final cadence. This practice promotes a more distinct articulation of phrasal structure, in keeping with the style of the period.
   - *Dynamics.* For the first time in music history, crescendos and decrescendos were actively employed by composers. Singers should not become too emotionally involved when they are performing these changes in loudness in order to preserve a controlled, objective mood. A good rule of thumb is to increase or decrease dynamics by no more than one level. As with Baroque music, dissonances need emphasis.
   - *Tempo.* Sensitivity to proper tempo is very important. When it is rushed, Classical period music tends to lose its stately character; when it is performed too slowly, its characteristic crispness and rhythmic vitality are lost. Pulsation is more gentle than that found in Baroque music and should not be "driven" excessively. A slight give-and-take in tempo was used, when influenced by the text, but was employed with restraint.

3. *Improvisation.* Ornamentation was still performed, but more moderately than in the Baroque period. Trills do occur frequently but are treated differently than the "prepared trills" of the Baroque period. (See Figure 9–4.) When you are using piano for accompaniment, embellishments should be performed less frequently than for harpsichord.

Figure 9–4

ROMANTICISM

In contrast to the relatively objective and formal nature of Classical period music, Romantic era works are generally more subjective and mood conscious. Unhampered by preconceived musical forms, the Romanticists concentrated more on pure sound by striving for unusual textures and sonorities. Dissonances were employed more frequently; extensive chromaticism and remote modulations began to push tonality toward its limit.

Lyricism continued to play an important role, as evidenced by the works of Schubert and others. Melody, however, also became more subservient to harmony, even losing its identity at times as it became engulfed within harmonically conceived dramatic action. Rhythm took on a more impetuous nature through frequent employment of syncopation, surges in tempo, and sudden accents.

1. *Performers.* Most of the Romantic period's choral repertoire is

intended for large performing forces and concert hall audiences. Berlioz' *Requiem* was first presented by nine hundred singers and instrumentalists. Many works, such as Beethoven's *Choral Symphony*, are primarily orchestral pieces requiring very large choruses for climactic impact.

But some Romanticists also wrote choral music of extraordinary beauty for more conservatively sized vocal groups. Many such works by Brahms are best performed by small chamber ensembles; motets by Bruckner fare better with somewhat larger forces. You should consider the expressive demands of these compositions on an individual basis when you are determining the appropriate number of singers.

2. *Stylistic requirements*
   * *Tonal color.* Expressive terms such as *con fuoco* (with fire) and *mesto* (sad) are indicative of the more emotional involvement required for the performance of Romantic period music. Singers need to produce a relatively more weighted and richer tonal quality. Beware, however, of oversinging, as evidenced by tense necks and, occasionally, red faces.
   * *Phrasing.* Phrases are often irregular and frequently unpredictable. Concise phrases may be followed by others that are extended through the use of deceptive cadences or even absorbed into new material. Therefore, considerably more flexibility in breathing will be required. The director's prime responsibility in this regard is to show singers how individual phrases are to be interpreted.
   * *Dynamics.* Changes in volume are sometimes abrupt and extreme. Dynamics may range from *pppp* to *ffff*, and a variety of levels are usually specified within a choral work. In these instances simply singing loudly or softly will not satisfy requirements. For this reason, plan to spend time with your ensemble developing a full repertoire of individual dynamic levels. Changes in loudness also require subjective involvement by the singers for full impact. Pianissimos are best performed with hushed intensity; sudden fortissimos should be unleashed with emotional vigor.
   * *Tempo.* Strictly regulated speed and moderate pace are not characteristic of the period. Terms such as *presto* and *molto lento* are common. Much of the choral repertoire requires a give-and-take in tempo. This is frequently requested by the composer in the form of accelerandos and ritardandos. In many other instances no markings are evident, yet some amount of phrasal freedom is

obviously necessary to breathe life into melodic lines. Tempo rubato is an important interpretive refinement not to be overlooked when you are performing Romantic period music.

3. *Interpretation*. Details in interpretive requirements differ among Romantic composers. For example, grace notes found in Schubert's vocal music are usually lengthened into eighth notes, whereas those encountered in Brahms' *Liebeslieder Waltzes* are performed more crisply so as not to interfere with the dance-like flow of the music. It is impossible to cover here the wide variety of interpretive nuances required for various composers' works. Score analysis will often reveal logical solutions. Critical listening of definitive performances will also lead to insights.

IMPRESSIONISM

During the late nineteenth and early twentieth centuries, the French movement called "Impressionism" produced, among other things, several significant choral works. The chief composer of this late Romantic period trend was Claude Debussy. Choral directors should also note the works of Ravel and Delius, an Englishman who wrote in the same style.

In contrast to the predominantly assertive nature of most nineteenth century works, Impressionistic music hints rather than states, often becoming preoccupied with dreamlike evocation of moods. Melodic lines usually tend to avoid sharp contour or strong sense of direction. Pentatonic and whole-tone scales are extensively employed for flavor as well as to avoid the decisiveness of tonality. Harmony is often nonfunctional, relying for its effect on unresolved dissonances and parallel movement of "gliding chords." Even rhythm is generally subdued and stripped of any sense of momentum.

1. *Performers*. Some Impressionistic works, such as Delius' *Sea Drift*, require full orchestra and chorus. More intimate choral chansons by Ravel and Debussy are intended for a cappella performance by chamber-sized groups.

2. *Stylistic requirements*
   * *Tonal color*. Discipline and restraint are prerequisites for properly performing Impressionistic music. Controlled soft singing, requiring continual breath support, will aid in this regard if it is practiced and incorporated into the repertoire at hand. Even crescendos and dynamic climaxes should be conditioned by this regulated approach. Vibrato may be allowed to color vocal performance as with Romantic period repertoire.

- *Phrasing.* Impressionistic music is, for the most part, very flowing. Phrases are often irregular or fragmented to achieve this effect. Therefore, legato singing and unobtrusive breathing must permeate interpretive performance. Occasional deviations toward crisper articulation, as required in the music, should be conditioned by this basically smooth mode of presentation.
- *Dynamics.* Color, rather than stress and accent, has priority. For this reason, dynamics are more subdued and require appropriate restraint.

3. *Interpretation.* Impressionistic music is refined in construction and expressive detail. A considerable amount of polishing time will be needed for developing interpretive nuance. Singers need to learn how to suggest rather than affirm in this style of musical expression.

TWENTIETH-CENTURY MUSIC

Choral literature from the modern era presents an unprecedented challenge for today's ensemble director. Unlike music of earlier periods, many contemporary compositions require their own unique stylistic interpretation. This is especially true where composers have made significant changes in their compositional style. Keeping in mind that a twentieth-century work must often be regarded as a law unto itself, you can still identify three general categories of choral repertoire requiring somewhat similar methods of interpretation.

Expressionism

Expressionistic music is for the most part atonal and usually implies the use of twelve-tone technique. Canonic devices, such as retrograde and inversion, are frequently used to present the original tone row in various forms. Representative choral composers are Schoenberg and Webern.

This type of music depends on distortion for its emotional impact. Excitement is created not only through pungent texts, but also by unusual musical surprises such as sporadic and unpredictable rhythms. Melodic lines often consist of jagged leaps distributed between vocalists and instrumentalists. Harmonic treatment is achieved primarily through the use of dissonant tone clusters.

1. *Performers.* Webern's cantatas are short, intensive works requiring chamber orchestra and small chorus for clarity. Stravinsky's *Threni*, on the other hand, is a more weighty composition, written for extensive

performing forces. Expressionistic music is very demanding of singers. Technically it calls for extensive vocal range and unusual flexibility. Musically it requires excellent ears to locate and hold onto seemingly unrelated pitches. Performance of this music should only be attempted by advanced ensembles.

2. *Stylistic requirements*
   - *Pitch.* Unless the composer requests *Sprechstimme* (song speech), pitches must be performed exactly as written, or the music will lose its integrity and sense of character. Clarity of individual tones is essential, so vibrato must be kept to a minimum. Abundant time must be provided for note learning until singers gain confidence in locating and holding their pitches. Choristers should be encouraged to sing with relaxed jaws when they are negotiating wide intervallic leaps.
   - *Phrasing.* Phrases are frequently constructed from strings of isolated notes and clusters distributed between various vocal parts and instruments in hocket style. Once the overall amount of give-and-take in rhythm and tempo has been determined for each phrase, performers must learn to come in at proper times so as not to destroy phrasal character.
   - *Dynamics.* Sudden gushes of loudness followed by retreats into softness permeate the Expressionistic repertoire. Singers should be prepared to explode dynamic climaxes when necessary.
   - *Tempo.* Speeds often fluctuate considerably over short spaces of time, a characteristic requiring flexibility on the part of the director and ready compliance by performers. In spite of highly angular vocal lines, rhythm must be scrupulously maintained, or the intensity in this type of music may be lost.

3. *Interpretation.* Expressionism often has a restless, even erotic quality which needs to be brought out in performance. Understanding and careful articulation of the text, with emotionalized emphasis of key words, will help in conveying appropriate mood.

Tonal-Oriented Music

A large proportion of twentieth century choral repertoire maintains some type of a relationship with tonality.

- Tonal-centered music creates a vague rather than definite sense of key.
- Polytonal music makes use of more than one key at the same time.

Common compositional devices encountered are primitive rhythms, chords built out of fourths, and jazz elements. Two compositional schools are represented within this category, each requiring somewhat different methods of interpretation.

Neoclassicism

In an attempt to avoid both the unrestrained emotion of Romanticism and the exaggerated distortion of Expressionism, some composers have combined contemporary technique with seventeenth and eighteenth century concepts and forms. Emphasis on craftsmanship and an objective style is usually the result. Contrapuntal composition, a prominent practice of this school, frequently employs harmonic dissonance through the use of highly independent lines. Rhythm plays an active, stylized role, as it did in the Classical period, but is often subjected to syncopation and metrical alteration. Leading composers of choral music in this style have included Stravinsky, Hindemith, Poulenc, and Britten.

1. *Performers.* Use of older genres such as the madrigal and cantata are indicative of the preference for smaller performing forces in Neoclassic music. Instruments are frequently placed in a chamber or solo role. Because of this increased responsibility, younger players may require additional guidance by the director.
2. *Stylistic requirements.* As with earlier period choral music, clarity of line is essential. Emotional expression should also be minimized in keeping with the more objective nature of this music.
3. *Interpretation.* Unlike Baroque and Classical period music, Neoclassic music provides little latitude for improvisation. Composers tend to specify their interpretive requirements with clarity and detail through the use of expressive terms and metronome markings.

Neoromanticism

Twentieth century composers have also taken a different direction by incorporating their contemporary techniques within more sonorous forms characteristic of the Romantic period. Neoromantic, also referred to as Post-romantic, choral works tend to emphasize textual content and subjective dramatic expression. A healthy proportion of this repertoire also contains elements of folk music, as exemplified by choral compositions of Kodály and Vaughan-Williams. Harmony is often of a less complex nature than harmony of late nineteenth century music. Yet it frequently produces rich colors with a sense of directness.

1. *Performers.* As in the Romantic period, choral works for large forces predominate. *Belshazzar's Feast* by William Walton, scored for double chorus, orchestra, and two brass bands, is a prime example. However, excellent compositions for smaller groups also exist, including an abundance of selections for men's and women's ensembles.

2. *Stylistic requirements.* Neoromantic compositions require warmth and subjective expression, in keeping with nineteenth century interpretive practice. Many of these works, especially those written for small groups, depend heavily on mood for their success. The director should carefully choose tempos which best capture the work's expressive qualities.

Experimental Music

All twentieth-century interpretive styles not previously discussed are included within this final category. Most experimental music places new and interesting demands on both conductor and performer. Some scores are complex and require considerable thought and conceptualization. New types of notation require explanation to the performers. Writings by the composer, whenever they exist, offer essential insights.

In some choral works singers may be required to choose their notes with certain latitude; in other instances individuals may perform their part with liberal freedom. Electronic music has also played an influential role in these types of choral compositions. Usually the choral group is backed in performance by electronic accompaniment played on a tape recorder.

1. *Performers.* Composers frequently leave ensemble size up to the director. This means that a particular work will take on different qualities depending on choice of performing forces. In these instances you should weigh the importance of clarity versus dynamic weight in determining the best solution for a particular work. Of course, other compositions may be more specific in their performance force requirements.

   Composers also write for unusual combinations of voices and instruments. For example, *The Odes of Shang* by Seymour Shiffrin requires an extensive battery of percussive instruments including wind chimes and gongs.

2. *Stylistic requirements.* Tonal colors may vary from absolutely straight tones to dark, resonant speaking sounds. Dynamics often range in

intensity from whispers to shouts. Here are some other types of sounds required in nonconventional scores:

- Laughter
- Screams
- Tongue clicks
- Hissing
- Hand claps

Encourage your singers to experiment and have a good time with these unorthodox sounds. During subsequent rehearsals you can channel their efforts toward performance requirements. When they are performing microtones or even minor seconds, singers have a natural tendency to match notes with each other because they have been conditioned by tonal music. Time must be spent teaching them how to select and maintain random pitches. A similar problem exists when they are attempting to perform irregular entries. Giving deliberately vague cues and showing individuals how to choose their own entries within time frames will help in this regard.

3. *Interpretation.* Because experimental music is so innovative, it is sometimes difficult to understand. Listeners must rely on effective performance if they are to gain an appreciation for this type of music. And successful presentations result only when singers are able to contribute with their understanding and commitment. Therefore, it is up to the director to provide the ensemble with a clear concept of an individual work's sense of purpose, mood, and format. Once this is established, performers must work with the director in experimenting with various types of articulation and timing until sounds, rhythmic patterns, and textures which best communicate the expressive content of a particular composition are found. (See Situation 9–B.)

SITUATION 9–B

Barbara L's singers were about to learn their first aleatoric work with electronic tape accompaniment. She played a recording of a similar type of composition, explaining its concept. The singers were impressed by the example's dramatic impact and became enthusiastic about their new piece of music.

CHAPTER 10

LEARNING MUSIC

Learning music is essentially a problem-solving activity. If treated as an obstacle to concert performance, singers will find your rehearsals tedious and boring. However, if you use the learning of music as an opportunity for discovery and growth, concerts will serve as culminating experiences within a vibrant, ongoing process. (See Situation 10–A.)

SITUATION 10–A

Shirley U. gets excited when she introduces a new choral work. She knows where note-learning difficulties will occur and offers appropriate solutions. Her singers characterize rehearsals as "adventures."

The learning of music should be conducted within a pre-established plan for each rehearsal. (See Chapter 6 for a "Planning Guide" for determining sequence of activities.)

ANALYZING THE SCORE

Before engaging in the actual teaching of music, the director must have a firm concept of a specific musical work's qualities. There are three reasons for this—

- To determine a work's salient features and convey this to the singers
- To perform the work in a manner compatible with the composer's intentions
- To determine potential score-learning difficulties

The choral director needs more information than the ensemble to be able to make decisions regarding learning and interpreting music. The degree and extent of information passed on to your singers will depend on such factors as level of understanding and available rehearsal time.

What the Score Communicates

The musical score is a visual representation of the composer's creative ideas. In many ways, it is similar to an architect's blueprint.

- It conveys an overall design or form.
- It shows the materials chosen and offers a view of their relationships.
- It indicates directions for actual implementation.

By examining the score, the choral director can determine the music's overall logic. Such insight is a prerequisite both for planning effective rehearsals and for performing the work with clarity and meaning.

The general character of a musical composition is determined by three elements:

- Function
- Form
- Sense of movement or direction

The work's specific character is influenced by the composer's choice of ingredients and a personalized treatment which makes the music truly unique. If the choral director is to gain a total understanding of these distinctive qualities, he or she must study the score in a process which moves from general familiarity to critical examination.

Becoming Acquainted With the Score

The familiarization phase begins even *before* the music is actually chosen for performance. Pre-selection factors such as repertoire need, available performers, and level of difficulty are considered. Reference copies are perused for textual content, individualistic features, and aesthetic impression. As a rule, the decision to perform any music should not be made until you have a clear picture of the work's actual suitability. This can be accomplished by studying the score silently, playing it on the keyboard, or listening to a recording.

After a choral composition has been chosen, the next step is to identify the following general features:

- Genre (madrigal or cantata, for example)
- General style (Renaissance or Classical, for example)
- Approximate performance time
- Meter
- Tempo

The third, and last, step in the initial familiarization phase is to determine the tonal structure of the work. Note that the word "key" is not used here, because much of the exciting choral music available for programming is written in "unconventional" sonoric idioms. The following is a list of tonal structures:

- Diatonic-major
- Diatonic-minor
- Modal
- Whole-tone
- Chromatic
- Atonal
- Polytonal (more than one key used *simultaneously*)
- Bifocal (*alternate* use of two keys)
- Tonal-centered (creates only a *general* sense of key)
- Migrantly-tonal (*alternate* use of tonality and atonality)
- Exotic

Examining the Score for Overall Form and General Content

In moving toward a more analytical phase, your next objective is to determine the work's basic construction. As in observing the layout of a building or the design of a product, this is achieved by locating sections and determining their relative proportions and substance. To assist in this process, a Form and Content Chart should be prepared. (See Figure 10–1.)

Lengthy choral works, such as oratorios, cantatas, and Masses, are usually composed in movements which should be compared for similarities and contrasts based on an analysis of each formal unit. Searching for sectional

FORM AND CONTENT CHART

Johannes Brahms. "Am Donaustrande," No. 9, from *Liebeslieder Walzer*, Op. 52

MEASURES	1–18=18	19–34=16	:35–47=13	48–62=15	63·64=2
METER	3/4				
TEMPO	"Ländler"				
KEY	E Major		B Major— g # minor	E Major	
TEXT	Am Donaustrande . . . . Mädchen aus.	Das Mädchen ist . . . . Türe gelegt.	Zehn eiserne . . . . von Glas.	Am Donaustrande . . . . Mädchen aus.	
MELODIC LINE	2-phrased melody	Same, but with modified ending	New melodic material	Original melody	
VOCAL FORCES	A, T, B		S, A, T, B	A, T, B	
ACCOMPANIMENT	Piano, for 4 hands Embellishing activity in upper part	Embellishing activity in lower part	Use of staccato in both parts	Embellishing activity shared between parts	
DYNAMICS	p		f	p	pp
SECTION DESIGNATOR	a	a	:b	a	: piano ending

FORM: Rounded binary, commonly known as minuet form.

Figure 10–1

changes within these movements and in shorter works is best achieved by observing the following warning signs:

- Changes in key, meter, and tempo
- Completion of a textual idea or narrative episode
- Introduction of a new theme or contrasting melodic material
- Logical groupings of musical phrases and final cadences
- Contrasting uses of rhythm and harmony
- Changes in performing forces

When you are constructing the Form and Content Chart, be sure that these indicators are also noted. They will help provide clues to the next step, which is to evaluate the chart and determine the score's overall formal design. If you compare sections for similarities and contrasts, the music will most likely fall into one of the following categories:

- Strophic (a a a. . .)
- Modified strophic (a a^1 a. . .)
- Variation (a a^1 a^2. . .)
- Stanza-refrain (a r b r. . .)
- Binary (|:a:|:b:|)
- Ternary (a b a)
- Rounded binary (|:a:|:ba:|)
- Rondo (a b a c a. . .)
- Imitative (fugue, canon)
- Through-composed (a b c d. . .)
- Modified through-composed (a b c a. . .)

Interpreting the Text

The text usually provides a composer with the initial inspiration to create a new choral work. In this respect, the words are really the "backbone" of the composition. An understanding of key words and phrases as well as a grasp of a work's textual message will often provide insights into the music's phrase structure and expressive meaning. Furthermore, this knowledge, if it is conveyed to the singers, will make the difference between mere transmission of sounds and communication of feeling.

This discussion recalls an interesting personal experience. I once presented a choral work, based on a well-known storybook subject, to my choir for learning. After the initial run-through, some of the members complained about the sinister text, the clashing dissonances, and the general somberness of the music. The choir returned to the composition with a new-found enthusiasm after they were given pertinent insight. What was the music? It was Irving Fine's witty setting of the "Lullaby of the Duchess" from *Alice's Adventures in Wonderland*.

Texts should be examined for the following characteristics:

- Relation of notation to text (syllabic, several notes per syllable, etc.)
- Continuity of text (fragmented, repeated, etc.)
- Inflection of text (normal or unusual stress of syllables, rise and fall of words within sentences, etc.)
- Clarity of text (clearly delineated by sparse use of rhythm, clouded by contrapuntal treatment, etc.)

If you choose to perform foreign languages, do not rely exclusively on free translations to interpret the text. Word-for-word, verbatim translations usually provide insights that most poetical translations overlook. The intimate relationship between word and music in foreign music can often be appreciated only by digging into a translation dictionary for exact meaning.

Introducing Character Analysis

The unique character of a composition may be traced to a particular device or element. But often it is a combination of features which determines this individuality. Only by systematically looking at all aspects of the composer's work will these character traits become evident.

Character Analysis is an organized method of examining all aspects of a musical work to determine its unique personality. Character analysis differs from theoretical analysis in that its goals are more performance oriented. If you follow its step-wise approach, a thorough understanding of the score is ensured.

To save time and minimize effort, the character analysis procedure is presented below. Four of the fundamental elements of music—sound (also called timbre), melody, harmony, and rhythm—provide the basic avenues of concentration in this practical approach. You should comb through the score for the information requested and make note of pertinent features. In some cases, the characteristic searched for will not exist. It must be kept in mind, however, that the features a work lacks as well as those it possesses are what gives a composition its distinctive character.

1. Analyze the overall sound
   - Unusual individual or group performing forces
   - Unusual individual or group ranges or extremes
   - Frequency of timbral contrasts (shifts from high to low performing forces, changes between different sounding combinations, for example)
   - Exploitation of singers or instruments for unusual effects
   - Types of articulation required (methods of attack, accentuation, etc.)
   - Types of dynamics indicated; choose from the following—terraced (abrupt), tapered (gradual), combination of the above
   - Frequency of implied dynamics resulting from addition or subtraction of performers or changes in range
   - Echo effects
   - Predominant dynamic level
   - Prevailing texture; choose from the following: homophony (chordal), true polyphony (contrapuntal), harmonically saturated polyphony, melody-bass polarity, or melody and accompaniment

2. Analyze the melodic content
   - Melodic design; choose from the following: motific (short, concise melodic figure), thematic (subject of fugue or complete musical idea), melodic (expanded linear material of three or more phrases), combination of the above
   - Overall profile, or contour, of the melodic design; evaluate for peaks and valleys
   - Characteristic motion of the melodic design; analyze for relative abruptness or gentleness in rise and fall
   - Prevalence of steps, skips, or leaps
   - Use of question (antecedent) phrases and answer (consequent) phrases

3. Analyze the harmony
   - General harmonic structure. Use the following procedure:
     a. Locate maximum harmonic tension and places of vertical complexity (active and dissonant chords, delayed resolutions, chord clusters, increased doubling, etc.)
     b. Locate areas of repose and vertical simplicity (final cadences, consonances, triads, minimal doubling, etc.)

- Characteristic harmonic rhythm (general rate of harmonic change)
- Use of compositional devices. Choose from the following: circle of fifths, ostinato patterns, pedal point, arpeggio treatment, raised and lowered thirds, or open (incomplete) chords
- Unusual doublings, inversions, and progressions
- Unusual implied harmonies

4. Analyze the rhythm
   - Relationship of pulsation (underlying level of temporal activity) to meter
   - Relationship between rhythm and meter. Choose from the following: Regular recurrence of rhythmic accent with metrical stress (isometrical rhythm), independent rhythm with little or no dependence on metrical organization (multimetrical rhythm), combination of the above
   - Use of polyrhythm (*simultaneous* employment of two or more *independent* rhythmic patterns)
   - Intensification and relaxation of rhythmic activity
   - Use of compositional devices. Choose from the following: augmentation, diminution, perpetual motion, rubato, hemiola, or syncopation
   - Relationship of rests to rhythmic structure
   - Types of stress. Choose from the following: natural (bar line), dynamic induced (accent markings), or combination of the above
   - Patterns of change in tempo and meter

Marking the Score

This last step in score progression is absolutely essential, for it allows you to clearly observe and communicate important information found on the printed page of music. Many directors, however, limit themselves by only using one color. When you employ various colors, you will be able to glance at your score and immediately see critical markings and other points of information.

Several color codes are possible. Once you have chosen a system, stay with it in all score markings and you will begin to react automatically to the various colors as they are approached in rehearsing or performing. I prefer the following color code:

1. *Yellow* is ideal for highlighting all tempo, metric, and key markings. It is also good for bringing out interpretation and articulation terms and markings.

2. *Blue* works well for various piano markings and decrescendos. I differentiate between levels of softness by varying the shape of my markings.

- (pp)
- (p)
- [mp]

3. *Red* is a logical choice for all forte markings and crescendos. The various levels of loudness can also be set off by varying the shape of your colored markings.

- [mf]
- (f)
- (ff)

4. *Black* is good for writing in additional information such as places for breathing or new markings. Word and note changes as well as phonetic markings should also be written in black. Any of these additions could, in turn, be highlighted in yellow for further clarity.

5. *Green* is especially useful for writing in performer cues. Reminders for changing lighting, seating singers, and so on can also be included.

TROUBLESHOOTING FOR POTENTIAL PROBLEMS

The effective choral director must anticipate potential problems encountered by singers learning and performing a musical work. This implies an intimate acquaintance with each vocal part and its relationship with other parts. The director must be prepared to either alleviate an anticipated obstacle completely or come up with a method for overcoming it with a minimum of rehearsal time and effort. Technical vocal problems are discussed in Chapter 8. Many problems, however, can be linked directly to the composition itself.

Choosing Proper Remedies

Providing the proper solution is as important to the troubleshooting process as locating the problem. Sometimes good intentions in pinpointing potential pitfalls are defeated by ineffectual solutions. The ability to match obstacles with suitable antidotes is a hard-earned skill requiring common sense, imagination, experience, and sometimes trial-and-error testing. The following are a few general guidelines:

- Adopt a clinical approach by choosing a tailor-made prescription for each problem.

- Isolate the components in complex problems and tackle each aspect individually.
- Choose vocal demonstration whenever possible.
- Minimize theoretical discussions. The ear works better than the word.

Potential problems often become evident as the score is analyzed for its form, general content, and character traits. Others must be discovered through concentrated troubleshooting. All tend to fall into three main categories:

- Reading problems
- Intonation problems
- Technical problems

Reading Problems

Many of the perplexities related to initial learning of music can be traced to score reading. In searching for possible solutions, you should ask four basic questions of the score.

1. *Does the printed music hinder the performer?* Despite the authority of the printed note, mistakes do occur. Some publishers, unfortunately, have a reputation for allowing such blemishes to creep into their music. A typical example occurs when a chromatically altered note is not changed in all performance lines. Often this discrepancy occurs between the choral parts and the accompaniment.

Awkward page turns sometimes cause inconveniences at first. Cautioning singers to place a finger at that point for a fast turn will solve the problem.

Occasionally, the notation or text is squeezed together to the point of creating a "sight-reading traffic jam." The only solution is to slacken tempo until the performers become more familiar with the score.

2. *Does the score contain places where the singers may lose their musical frame of reference?* Much has been written about difficulties in sight-reading. Most occur simply because the singer does not sense the relationship of his or her part to the total ensemble. Finding initial pitches, modulating to new keys, and confidently progressing through dissonances can only be achieved when the performers hear their parts contextually.

The role of the choral director in providing musical reference points cannot be overstressed. Sometimes this may mean locating common tones between two parts; in other instances, clarifying harmonic progressions will help. Often these reference points can only be discovered by patiently studying the score.

3. *Is the music unpredictable?* Altered sequences, sudden contrasts in harmonic treatment, and abrupt dynamics are examples of favorite compositional surprises. Singers will sometimes fall into these musical pitfalls unless they are forewarned.

4. *Are there speed traps?* Highly energized rhythmic passages such as those typically found in Baroque contrapuntal music pose sight-reading obstacles to the average singer. Chordal music marked by unrestful skips and leaps within vocal lines pose similar problems. Generally speaking, clusters of short-durational notes, busy chromatic activity, and intensified vertical movement indicate speed traps. The solution? Treat the tempo conservatively at first.

Intonation Problems

Pitch problems caused by faulty vocal technique and hearing are discussed in Chapter 8. Intonation is also affected by acoustic conditions created by the musical composition.

1. *Look for individual notes which control tonal structure.* Leading tones, especially when they are employed for modulation to a new key, cannot be allowed to sag. The third of a chord must be sung with precision because it determines the mode of the chord. Notes which change the character of a sequence are also important. If not performed properly, sequential passages will sound muddy and ambiguous.

2. *Treat unison passages with caution.* From the standpoint of pitch, a choral ensemble is *naked* whenever it performs music in unison or at the octave. Watch for cadences ending with such treatment.

Technical Problems

These obstacles range from simple clarification of musical terminology to matters of synchronization. Technical problems tend to fall into the following three categories:

1. *Problems in clarification.* What does *"Bocca chiusa"* mean? How does one perform a Baroque trill? Scores are often filled with symbols and directions unfamiliar to the choral member. Based on a knowledge of your group, you must be prepared to provide information and insights to the

extent that all musical data contained in the composition can be translated into accurate performance.

2. *Breathing problems.* Every score requires a "plan of attack" for breathing. Nothing destroys the momentum or mood of a work more than obtrusive sounds of rushing air in the wrong places. A lengthy musical arc may demand staggered breathing. Conversely, the repetition of a text statement or an individual word may require interjection of breaths or pauses. The conscientious director will test his or her breathing plan by singing through the score *before* presenting it to the ensemble.

3. *Coordination problems.* All music contains primary and subsidiary activity. For example, the subject of a fugue is passed about while other voices provide the countersubject or free material. The discerning director must plan to control performance balances based on an analysis of this musical activity. Duplicate responses require equal balance. Yet, if the chorus is hampered by unequal vocal strength between sections of the ensemble, modification of dynamics or substitution of voices may be necessary.

Troubleshooting may also reveal relatively independent movement between vocal lines. Renaissance madrigals characteristically employ this treatment. Be sure that this type of music does not "loosen at the seams" by carefully regulating the tempo.

NOTE LEARNING AND TECHNICAL MASTERY

In Chapter 6 the preparation of a choral work was described as a three-phase process:

- Note-learning and technical mastery
- Polishing
- Interpreting

This, of course, does not imply that you should come to a screeching halt in the middle of a rehearsal because a certain phase has just been completed, nor does it mean that all selections should reach the same stage at exactly the same time. The transition into a new phase should be fluid and natural, with considerable overlapping caused by differences in the demands of each choral work.

Leonhard and House describe the best way to begin learning music in their highly regarded book, *Foundations and Principles of Music Education.*[1]

---

[1]Charles Leonhard and Robert W. House, *Foundations and Principles of Music Education* (2nd ed.; New York: McGraw-Hill Book Company, 1972), p. 287.

The process of teaching music has been analyzed as a three-phase pattern of (1.) synthesis, (2.) analysis, and (3.) synthesis.

This approach has been proven to be particularly suitable for teaching choral repertoire. Your task is to guide the ensemble through each step, using teaching strategies and learning aids necessary to best accomplish the job.

Synthesis

Choral directors sometimes make the mistake of picking apart a work right from the beginning. (See Situation 10–B.) The trouble with this approach is that performers never gain an overview or perspective until after the music has been learned. Insight saves time!

Begin by providing any background information you can offer about the selection. This may mean translating part of a foreign text, defining the genre of the work, or even informing your choir about the original purpose of the composition. Besides helping to "sell" the work, this initial orientation can be important in establishing the group's attitude towards the score.

Now, the ensemble is ready to make its first acquaintance with the actual music. Somehow the singers need to become initially familiar with the entire composition. This is usually accomplished through sight-reading, but there are other effective methods.

1. *Scanning.* Rather than reading each and every note, the choral group looks through the score as the director points out form, contrasts in compositional technique, unifying or recurring material, and so on. Portions of the score should be sung in the initial perusal. This approach is especially suitable for large, multi-sectional works.

2. *Demonstration.* Another obvious method is to play a recording of the music, if available. For extended-length works, this may necessitate playing individual sections during several rehearsals. Sometimes a core of good sight-readers or singers who have previously performed the selection can be used for demonstration.

3. *Singing with a recording.* Some purists might look down on this method. There are instances, however, when singing along with a record or tape recording will save valuable rehearsal time. One interesting innovation is the use of a quadrophonic tape system. Each individual line in four-part music can be prerecorded, either by keyboard or singer, on one of four tracks. Vocal sections then group themselves in front of the appropriate loudspeaker and are able to hear and perform their part contextually. This approach is very useful for learning difficult contemporary music.

SITUATION 10–B

Sam F. liked to work phrase-by-phrase with his church choir right from the beginning. The trouble was, by the time his choristers reached the end of the anthem, they had forgotten what they had learned in the beginning.

Analysis

At this point, the singer is ready to become absorbed in a detailed study of the music. The conscientious conductor has already prepared the score and noted likely places of difficulty. Now he or she is ready to solve note learning problems through a process of what I call "compartmentalization." Simply put, this means isolating problems and removing as many extraneous factors as possible. For example, if singers are having rhythmic difficulties, slowing the tempo and eliminating the text will allow them to concentrate on their problem. Speaking a neutral syllable on the same pitch would simplify learning conditions even more since the factor of pitch recognition would also be eliminated. The following are more examples of compartmentalization:

- When *pitch problems* occur within homophonic (chordal) music, direct singers to perform each chord slowly and without regard to exact rhythm or meter so they can locate their pitches contextually

- Correct *rhythmic difficulties* by clapping. This is especially useful when polyrhythms occur between vocal sections

In conjunction with compartmentalization, choose teaching strategies which will help the singer correct errors. Compartmentalization *isolates* the problem; employing proper strategies helps *solve* the problem. Those most frequently employed in learning choral music are the following:

1. *Trial and error.* Many sight-reading mistakes are corrected by repetition; more serious errors require special attention. The effective director knows how to differentiate one from the other. Solve simple problems by trial and error.

2. *Listen and sing.* Most mistakes occur because the singer does not have a mental concept of the correct solution. Often, hearing the trouble spot played or performed by a demonstrator will help. The singer should then immediately perform the music to solidify the image.

3. *Elemental commonality.* Rarely does one encounter choral music where vocal parts share absolutely no relationship with each other. Elements of commonality often include melodic themes, rhythmic patterns, and text. Considerable time and effort will be saved by rehearsing vocal sections together whenever they share similar musical content.

   - When you are teaching contrapuntal music, have everyone sing subjects, countersubjects, and recurring episodic material in unison.
   - Whenever problems occur because of harmonic *dissonance*, rehearse those vocal parts together which share the most harmonic *consonance*.

4. *Superimposition.* Sometimes individual sections need to hear their music against the background of the other parts. This is best achieved by requesting the problem vocal section to perform at a relatively strong dynamic level while the volume of all other parts is suppressed.

5. *Wrong-right.* Occasionally, performers insist on singing the wrong notes in spite of repeated attention to the problem. This may be caused by an unnatural melodic line or awkward intervals. Usually, however, the difficulty results from a mental block. In these cases, instruct the vocalists to perform the music alternately correctly and incorrectly. By rejecting the incorrect version and approving the proper response, you will help them overcome their problem through reinforcement.

6. *Intervallic.* Whenever singers have difficulty with a particular interval in their music, require them to perform that interval several times in various keys. Then, return to the music and hope for improvement.

Synthesis

The final stage in the music learning process can be compared to putting together a jigsaw puzzle. As each musical section becomes eligible for graduation from the analysis stage, it receives a trial run-through. A cappella performance is especially useful as a test to see if the ensemble can hold its own. Completed sections are then added together until the entire choral work has been learned.

Do not, however, always assemble sections according to their compositional order. Start with the most difficult places first since they take longer to shape up. I prefer a strategy which gives priority to analyzing and assembling musical sections according to their relative difficulty. This allows me to complete the work without spending an inordinate amount of rehearsal time on easier sections.

Technical Mastery

In most instances singers learn to accommodate vocal demands made by
the music as they become accustomed to their part. Warm-up exercises
devised from actual musical passages found within the music are especially
helpful. Technical mastery is a process which takes place at all stages of
learning music.

Sometimes, however, singers will need special assistance in meeting the
vocal demands of music they are learning. Here are some examples:

1. *Unusually high notes.* Ask singers to "darken" their vowels to create
   more space in the pharynx. For example, the *ee* vowel should be sung
   as *ih*. If singers are unsure of notes, have them sing high notes an
   octave lower until they are confident.

2. *Loud passages.* Emphasize the value of resonation as opposed to
   shouting. Demonstrate how a bigger sound can be achieved by
   opening up the back of the throat. Get singers to "yawn" out their
   vowels.

3. *Sustained legato singing.* Demand abundant support. Make sure jaws
   are relaxed.

4. *Rapid melismatic singing.* Choose a more moderate tempo at first to
   ensure that each note is articulated. Then speed up, making sure that
   singers' diaphragms are activated.

Pacing and variety are essential to achieving technical mastery. For
example, spending an inordinate amount of time on a vocally demanding
section will create undue fatigue. By providing brief periods of vocal rest
within the rehearsal and moving from one type of repertoire to another, you
will encourage beneficial development.

FEELING RHYTHM THROUGH BODY MOVEMENT

Proper execution of rhythm is only achieved when actually *felt* by your
singers. Jacques-Dalcroze formulated a system called "eurhythmics" emphasizing rhythm as the key to total musical development and its improvement
through body movement.[2] Rhythmic movement is particularly appropriate
for amateur musicians. It allows them to experience correct rhythms without

---

[2]This concept is stressed in Emile Jacques-Dalcroze's book *Rhythm, Music and
Education*, trans. Harold F. Rubinstein (New York: J.P. Putnam's Sons, 1921).

becoming preoccupied with technical understanding. Furthermore, you will gain two desirable side effects by involving singers in physical activities:

- They will "loosen up" and sing with more vocal freedom.
- They will develop a more cohesive interdependence between themselves.

Body Movement Exercises

1. Meter
   a. Maintaining a steady meter
      - For duple meter, singers sway entire body from left to right as though imitating a bell.
      - Singers describe a circle with their arms while clapping metrical patterns.
      - Singers walk while singing music, first in a circular movement, later, freely. Clapping of each beat may later be added.
   b. Metrical division
      - Singers march to metrical beats, accenting the first beat of each measure by stomping their foot.
   c. Metrical changes
      - For movement between 4/4 and 3/4, singers step to 4/4. At change to 3/4, they waltz alone or in couples. Process is reversed for movement back to 4/4.

2. Tempo
   a. Accelerando and decelerando changes
      - Singers adjust their rate of walking while performing changes in tempo. Short running steps may be required for faster tempos.
   b. Adjustments to distinct tempo changes
      - Conductor sets various tempos. Singers swing their arms while remaining in place, keeping torso free and loose.

3. Rhythm
   a. Specific rhythmic problems
      - Conductor claps pattern. Singers imitate with their hands, later with their feet.
   b. Syncopation
      - Conductor establishes an even tempo. Singers walk in syncopation. Their arms maintain the original beat pattern.
   c. Rests
      - Conductor speaks or plays a rhythmic pattern which contains rests. Singers clap rests only.

CHAPTER 11

POLISHING AND INTERPRETING MUSIC

Once music has been learned and placed in the voices, you are ready to begin the refinement process leading to concert performance. I find the second phase, polishing music, to be an appropriate time for improving diction.

CHORAL DICTION

Diction, as related to singing, is so important that entire books have been written on the subject. If there is one element which "separates the sheep from the goats" in terms of choral expressiveness, it is diction. According to Van A. Christy, "Proper attention to this one element can make a surprisingly good chorus from mediocre talent."[1] The purpose of this discussion is to emphasize those factors which contribute to good diction and to suggest some directions to take when you are attempting to improve your ensemble's treatment of a text.

The Necessity of Specialized Study

Choral directors need to study basic principles of diction and should have the ability to at least pronounce commonly used languages accurately. While attending the Juilliard School, I was required to study English, Italian, German, and French diction for one year each. Yet, in spite of this concentrated effort, I know that continuing education is a must. In order to effectively aid your ensemble with diction and textual interpretation, you should become proficient in the following areas:

- Knowledge of the International Phonetic Alphabet (IPA), including its symbols

- Ability to pronounce IPA sounds accurately

- Mechanistic knowledge of articulation (shape of the mouth, position of the tongue) in order to pronounce all the vowels, consonants, and diphthongs

---

[1]Van A. Christy, *Glee Club and Chorus* (New York: Schirmer Books, division of Macmillan Publishing Co., Inc., 1940). p. 44.

- Ability to pronounce all words accurately in choral works selected for performance
- Knowledge of natural stresses and elisions (slurring) inherent in each language
- Ability to translate foreign texts, including a basic knowledge of sentence structure

The Reasons for Good Choral Diction

Knowing why proper diction is important will help you to channel your efforts when you are working with ensemble singers. Good diction is necessary for the following reasons:

1. *To improve tone quality.* Vowels are the vehicles of tone quality, and any improvement in them will have a beneficial effect on the choir's vocal sound. Properly enunciated consonants help to focus vowels.

2. *To give coherence to the text.* Listeners who understand the language your ensemble is performing should be able to *comprehend* the textual content of each choral work.

3. *To avoid regional dialects.* Choral repertoire is international in scope and does not benefit by the addition of such ingredients as Bronx accents or Texas drawls.

4. *To give performances a more polished effect.* The audience may not understand your foreign languages, but they will know the difference between sloppy and precise articulation of words.

Proper Pronunciation

Pronunciation refers to accuracy of diction. The following types of errors frequently occur:

1. *Use of the wrong vowel.* Singers sometimes forget to change their pronunciation of the definite article "the" when it precedes a vowel. Failure to differentiate between the open and closed versions of a vowel is another problem.

A vowel chart developed by Alexander Graham Bell is particularly useful for improving accurate pronunciation of vowels. (See Figure 11–1.)

Once singers learn to associate each vowel with its number on the chart, you do not have to write symbols on the chalk board. If a large

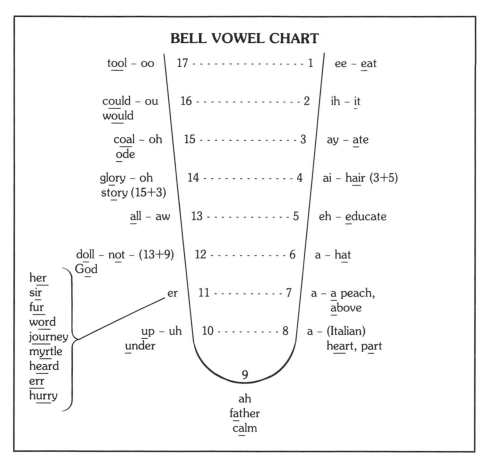

BELL VOWEL CHART

Figure 11–1

mock-up of the Bell Vowel Chart is permanently displayed at the front of the rehearsal room, you can call out vowel numbers and make instant spot corrections.

2. *Careless substitution of one consonant for another.* In an effort to bring out the final consonant in the word "eyes," your performers may fall into the trap of singing "ice." This is just one example of consonants pronounced differently from their appearance in print. How should the German word *"ewig"* be sung?

Consonants are either voiceless or voiced. A voiceless consonant requires aspiration (blowing of air) without sound; a voiced consonant is achieved by sound instead of aspiration. With the exception of *h*, each voiceless consonant has a corresponding voiced consonant. (See Figure 11–2.)

PAIRED CONSONANTS

Voiceless	*Voiced*
t	d
f	v
p	b
k	g (go)
th (as in thin)	th (thine)
s	z
sh	s (measure)
ch	j
	g (George)
wh	w

Figure 11–2

The following voiced consonants, however, do not have a corresponding voiceless sound: *r, y* (*you*), *m, n, ng* (*sing*), and *l*.

3. *Improper treatment of diphthongs.* A diphthong consists of two consecutive vowel sounds within the same syllable. Singers residing in the southern part of the country sometimes have a tendency to avoid the second vowel in certain diphthongs. The word "thy" becomes "thah." On the other hand, vocalists performing in a popular style often exaggerate the wrong vowel, and words such as "try" become "traheeee."

Diphthong vowels should not be treated equally. The *sustaining* vowel takes approximately nine-tenths of the total diphthong sound. This means the *vanishing* vowel will utilize only one-tenth of the total sound. Figure 11–3 presents the five principal diphthongs found in the English language. Note that sustaining vowels are underlined and vanishing vowels are placed in parentheses.

4. *Avoidance of the neutral vowel.* Also known as "schwa," the "uh" sound holds an important place in English, French, and German pronunciation. Please keep in mind that the neutral vowel is necessary to give coherence to texts and can be sustained in singing like other vowels. All four *e* vowels in the French excerpt ". . . comme ce cygne qui nage. . .," taken from Hindemith's chanson, *En Hiver* should be performed as neutral vowels.

```
┌─────────────────────────────────────────────────────────────┐
│              PRONUNCIATION OF DIPHTHONGS                     │
│                                                             │
│       IE as in LIE        =    AH   +   (EE)                │
│       OY as in TOY        =    AW   +   (EE)                │
│       OW as in NOW        =    AH   +   (OO)                │
│       EW as in FEW        =    (EE)  +   OO                 │
│       AY as in MAY        =    EH   +   (EE)                │
│                                                             │
└─────────────────────────────────────────────────────────────┘
```

Figure 11–3

```
┌─────────────────────────────────────────────────────────────┐
│           WORDS CONTAINING NEUTRAL VOWELS                   │
│                                                             │
│      angel           foreign          comfort              │
│      Christmas       ocean            murmur               │
│      never           passion          riot                 │
│      menace          treasure         handsome             │
│      heaven          autumn           homeward             │
│                                                             │
└─────────────────────────────────────────────────────────────┘
```

Figure 11–4

Figure 11–4 presents examples of neutral vowels given in italics.

5. *Mispronunciation of prefixes.* When ending in *e*, prefixes are sometimes pronounced inaccurately. It may be appropriate to "deefrost"
   your refrigerator, but can you imagine what it would be like to meet
   an audience that was "deelighted" by your concert? Remember the
   following rules:

   • The prefix *de* should be pronounced *dih* unless it refers to
     severance (the train was "deerailed"; the dog was "dihvoted.")
   • The prefix *re* should be pronounced *rih* unless it means a
     repetition of an action. (The trunk was "reepacked"; the song was
     "rihmembered.")

Improving Enunciation

Enunciation refers to the clarity with which words are pronounced or,
put in choral language, "getting the words across to the audience." (See
Situation 11–A.)

SITUATION 11–A

Joyce T. has a wonderful method for improving word clarity. Whenever her chorus mumbles their words, she imitates them with comic exaggeration. They improve instantly.

Here are some typical problems.

1. *Sloppy enunciation of initial and final consonants.* Watch especially for *d, t, h, k,* and *p.*

2. *Too much emphasis of the American* r. This results in a gargled sound and lack of authenticity in the case of foreign languages. Show singers how to flip or roll the *r* where necessary. Generally, the *r* should be eliminated when falling before a consonant in English texts. ("Hark" should be sung "hahk.")

3. *Tendency to lose clarity of diction when performing softly.* Although vowels can carry well in *pianissimo* singing, consonants need *forte* treatment at all times.

Enunciation is greatly influenced by the type of articulation found in the music.

1. *Legato style.* When musical lines are to be performed smoothly, singers should avoid "exploding" their consonants. Attaching consonants to vowels which *follow* will achieve smoother elision between syllables. (Christmas tree should be enunciated Chrih-smuh-stree.)

2. *Staccato style.* When musical lines are to be performed choppily, words should be more detached. Final *d, b,* and hard *g* preceding a consonant or pause should be enunciated clearly. Initial and final sibilants such as *s* and *z* should be crisply articulated.

3. *Marcato style.* When notes are accented or rhythms are heavily emphasized, words need to be exploded with force. The "Hallelujah Chorus" from Handel's *Messiah* is a good example because it requires forceful expiration of the syllable "hah."

COORDINATING THE ENSEMBLE

Let's assume that your choral group has learned the notes of a new score, can "hit" all of the notes well, and can convey the text with accuracy and clarity. Would you say that the musical work is ready for concert performance? If you answer yes, then you probably also believe that a successful football team is comprised of eleven lonely individuals doing separate tasks.

Choral performance requires *teamwork*. And this can only be achieved through careful coordination of individual, sectional, and overall group efforts with the conductor's intentions. For this phase of musical preparation, I find a "Polishing Checklist" to be invaluable. While you are rehearsing the choral work, listen critically for each checklist category and take corrective action to remedy problems.

POLISHING CHECKLIST

1. Attacks and releases
    a. Standard: uniform precision in ensemble execution
    b. Corrective actions:
        • Insist on eye contact.
        • Clarify pronunciation at attack and release points.
        • Isolate and rehearse separately problematic attacks and releases.

2. Breathing
    a. Standard: total compliance with the established breathing plan
    b. Corrective actions:
        • Insist on breathing only at designated places.
        • Stress need for adequate inhalation and controlled emission of breath.
        • Deliberately slow down demanding phrases to develop stamina and pacing.
        • Make sure that singers do not breathe in obtrusive places when they are employing staggered breathing.

3. Intonation
    a. Standards:
        • Accurate and timely movement to pitches especially within chords
        • Consistent preservation of pitch and key within each vocal section
    b. Corrective actions:
        • Insist on proper posture and adequate support.
        • Keep ensemble vocal production lyrical and forward in placement. Avoid chesty, throaty singing.
        • Make sure vowels are correctly and uniformly pronounced.

- Guard against "dipping" into successive notes on the same pitch.
- Beware of ensemble tendency to overstep descending intervals and understep ascending intervals.
- Avoid "key fatigue" from singing in one key too long.
- Experiment with raised and lowered keys, especially when a particular vocal section appears to have tessitura or register problems.
- Vary accompaniment by having the keyboard played an octave higher or lower or by using staccato.
- For accompanied choral works, switch to a cappella performance to develop ensemble pitch awareness.
- Make sure outer vocal parts are tuned and then tune inner parts.

4. Tonal intensity
   a. Standard: continued vibrancy of tone
   b. Corrective actions:
      - Insist on energized consonants and rounded vowels to prevent "dead" tones.
      - Stress the necessity for increased support when singers are singing softly.
      - Ask for a "hushed" rather than a soft response.
      - Strive for controlled, resonant singing of loud passages. Do not permit shouting or blatancy.

5. Rhythm and tempo
   a. Standards:
      - Precise execution of note values
      - Accurate initiation and maintenance of conductor's tempo
   b. Corrective actions:
      - Do not accept rhythmic discrepancies between individual singers.
      - To define exact moment of entry for each note, request choir to perform music staccato.
      - Practice the opening measure of the composition at various speeds to establish ensemble compliance.
      - When you encounter difficulty in maintaining a steady tempo, ask the singers to pulsate their music by accenting each pulse beat while singing.

6. Dynamics
   a. Standards:
      - Observance of all dynamic markings
      - Clarity of contrast between dynamic levels
      - Smooth control of crescendos and decrescendos
   b. Corrective actions:
      - Clarify which dynamic levels are required and then move to each marking and rehearse for accuracy in volume.
      - Verbally warn singers of upcoming dynamic markings as they perform the music.
      - Specify exactly where crescendos and decrescendos begin and end. For extended ones, ask singers to write in dynamic levels as signposts above designated notes.

7. Articulation
   a. Standards:
      - Observance of all articulation markings
      - Clarity of contrast between required articulations
   b. Corrective actions:
      - Demonstrate required articulations. Show the difference between accents and stresses, staccato and marcato, etc.
      - Verbally warn singers of upcoming articulations as they perform the music.

8. Blend
   a. Standards: uniformity of ensemble sound; no voices stick out
   b. Corrective actions:
      - Insist on a smooth, composite sound, especially when vocal sections have "solos."
      - Avoid edgy or "pinched" tone quality. Request singers to incorporate a "yawn" feeling into their singing.
      - Work with sections down to quartets or even to duets to achieve uniformity of sound.
      - Tactfully modify individual response if it destroys ensemble blend.

9. Balance
   a. Standards:
      - General equalization of tonal weight between vocal sections
      - Sectional sensitivity to dynamic give-and-take when required in the music

   b. Corrective actions:
- To achieve equal weight, require all sections to match volume with that produced by the *weakest* vocal part.
- Specify places where musical material should be brought out or subordinated by individual sections.
- To promote awareness of give-and-take in rehearsal, instruct performers to sing words only when they are presenting thematic material. Otherwise, when presenting subsidiary material, they should hum or sing a specified vowel.

DEVELOPING EXPRESSIVITY

Have you ever ordered the specialty of the house at a gourmet restaurant only to discover that the entree was undercooked? Such an experience can be particularly frustrating when you consider the time and energy that was necessary to prepare that delicacy—not to mention the expenditure of your money. Unfortunately, choral concerts are sometimes marred by "undercooked" presentations. The true flavor of a musical work can only be brought to fruition through that final phase called interpretation.

What Is Interpretation?

Interpretation refers to the creative art of bringing out a musical work's expressive qualities. Interpretation is achieved in several ways:

- By attempting to perform the work with stylistic accuracy (See Chapter 9.)
- By cultivating expression of the text
- By observing the music's expressive features
- By carefully adding subjective nuances to further enhance the music's expressivitiy

Cultivating Expression of the Text

When you bring out the meaning of texts which have been well set to music, the interpretive and expressive qualities of the music itself will begin to emerge. This is primarily achieved by emphasizing important words and stressing key syllables. Regardless of language, look for the following textual clues:

- Verbs expressing strong feeling or action (love, fight)

- Descriptive adjectives (beautiful, strong)
- Subjects and objects

Have your singers underline the syllables of words which need to be stressed and then practice reading the text while incorporating these stresses. Text "painting" may also be achieved by "leaning" on certain consonants.

- Final *m* or *n* in a musical phrase may be prolonged.
- Initial consonants may be held slightly longer for dramatic impact (save, weak).

Vowels may be modified to give emotional meaning to key words. Emotions such as anger or sorrow can be achieved by "coloring" vowel sounds. For example, a "great king" can be made to sound more impressive by "mixing" the darker "uh" sound with the diphthong "*EH* + (*EE*)" found in the word "great." According to Gordon Lamb,

The choral director should not be timid about using his musical ear as a guide to the modification of vowel sounds. At the same time, any coloring must be done with taste, and with concern that all of the choir is doing it together and to the same degree.[2]

Observing the Music's Expressive Features

Performing music with expressivity is synonymous with good musicianship. The difference in choral music is that the director must find ways to achieve this through the singers regardless of their present musical status. Locating expressive features is best achieved in conjunction with score analysis (see Chapter 10). The next step is to convey these insights to your ensemble and then devise methods to bring out the expressive features. The following suggestions may be useful:

1. Get singers to feel rhythm as dynamic *movement* through time.
   - Long notes need to be "sung through" rather than simply "held."
   - Rests need to be "performed silently" rather than simply "counted."
2. Outline the contour of important musical phrases on a chalkboard.
   - Show where points of tension and repose occur. Demonstrate how these points can be expressed through vocal intensity and tempo rubato.

---

[2]Gordon H. Lamb, *Choral Techniques* (2nd ed.; Dubuque: William C. Brown, 1979). p. 73.

- Show where give-and-take recurs *between* vocal lines—how balance may change continually between parts. Rehearse phrases individually, then put together.

3. Isolate individual chords, phrases, and sections which demand contrasting or unusual tonal expression.

- Discuss "marriages" inevitably occuring between important words and sound structure.
- Demonstrate the desired effect and rehearse performers for compliance.

Adding Subjective Nuances

Regardless of how specific a composer attempts to be regarding the interpretation of his or her music, subjective decisions must be made by the choral director. Just how long is that fermata? How long should one pause between movements? Although there are no correct answers for these types of decisions, there is an important factor to consider—"taste." According to the *Harvard Dictionary of Music,*

A personal interpretation is the performer's great privelege, granted him by the composer. A really fine performer is always aware of the responsibility toward the work that this privilege imposes.[3]

Be careful not to take excessive license with the work you are interpreting. Watch especially for the following undesirable tendencies:

- Cosmetic additions of expressive devices.
- Broadening of natural give-and-take within phrases into distinct accelerandos and decelerandos
- Drastic changes of tempo and dynamics

Knowing just how much and what kind of personal interpretation to add comes partly from experience. But it also comes from experiencing *others'* performance. By attending concerts, the visiting director can compare interpretations. Performing either as a soloist or in a choral ensemble is also helpful for developing a perspective and sensitivity for music's expressive qualities.

---

[3]"Interpretation", *Harvard Dictionary of Music*, Willi Apel, ed., (Cambridge, MA: The Belknap Press of Howard University Press, 1970.) p. 418.

CHAPTER 12

PREPARING FOR PERFORMANCE

Would you place an expensive painting in a cheap picture frame? Probably not, because a work of art requires a proper setting. Quality choral concerts can also be works of art. Yet, they are sometimes marred by "improper settings" caused by insufficient ensemble preparation, incomplete planning, or faulty coordination.

COMPLETING ENSEMBLE PREPARATION

I personally find the last rehearsals before performance to be the most fruitful and rewarding. This final period should be a time for eliminating last-minute problems, pulling everything together, and building confidence. If events are planned properly, your singers should "peak" at concert time. They should be neither under- nor over-rehearsed.

Memorization

There are several arguments for and against the performance of choral music from memory.

1. Advocates point out that singers are free to maintain continual eye contact with the director. The ensemble also makes a neater appearance without printed music, which tends to clutter the stage.

2. Those not in favor feel that time spent memorizing the music could be better applied to improving the vocal group's ability to perform the work. Musical errors caused by memorizing are also eliminated.

There are other factors to be considered when you are deciding whether or not the choir should memorize its music. Staging your group and planning for considerable movement or using a darkened stage to create special effects would dictate performing without printed music. On the other hand, memorization of atonal choral works or very lengthy oratorios would be difficult and time consuming.

If you choose to have music performed from memory, consider these suggestions.

1. Begin the memorization process when polishing and interpreting music; do not wait until the last rehearsals.

2. Use an *ABA* approach
   a. Singers perform a single page or section while looking at the printed score.
   b. They close their score and perform this material from memory. (For a cappella music, it is best to have an accompanist play during this phase to avoid possible "breakdowns.")
   c. After this, the singers immediately return to the printed score and perform the music a third time, making spot corrections of any mistakes or memory lapses that occurred.

3. As an alternative method, have half of the ensemble sing from memory while the other half reads from the score; then, reverse the two groups.

4. Divide the singers into sextettes or octets and assign them the responsibility of memorizing their music outside of rehearsal.

5. Set a good example by making sure that *you* have memorized the score.

6. Do not neglect previously memorized music. Periodically review those older works. This saves the time needed to memorize an entire score.

Stamina

Performing a lengthy concert under hot lights requires strength and endurance. For unconditioned singers, a performance may begin as an artistic experience but degenerate into an uncomfortable ordeal. Then the ensemble becomes plagued by sagging pitches and loss of musical vitality. Take the following steps to build stamina:

1. Approximately two weeks before a concert, ask singers to stand for part of the rehearsal. Increase this with each rehearsal until they have become accustomed to standing for the entire rehearsal several days prior to the performance. Show them how to avoid rigidity without detracting from their concert appearance by wiggling their toes, breathing for relaxation, and so on. This will also help to prevent fainting spells.

2. As the performance date approaches, allow the ensemble to perform single works, and then groups of compositions without interference. Only in this way will the choir members learn how to pace themselves or develop an ability to recover quickly from musical errors. Choral groups not achieving a

sense of continuity run the risk of losing poise and momentum if something goes wrong. (See Situation 12–A.)

SITUATION 12–A

Christopher W. would not allow a mistake to occur without stopping immediately for corrections—even during dress rehearsals. His concerts were marred frequently by breakdowns.

---

3. Build vocal stamina by encouraging choral members to sing at concert hall volume before the date of the performance.

4. If music is to be held, make sure that folders are kept at the proper height during rehearsals to build arm strength.

Sitting, Standing, and Moving

Formations and movements need to be worked out as much as possible before the dress rehearsal. If risers will be used for the concert, try to get the ensemble on them at this point, even if it means lugging them into your rehearsal room or spending part of rehearsal times using them on stage.

If chairs will be used on stage, now is the time to rehearse sitting and standing to develop uniformity of movement. It would also be beneficial to practice the actual movement on and off risers, back and forth to seats, etc. to develop a sense of flow and pacing.

Some choir directors overlook the creative possibilities for movement *within* and *between* musical selections. Even in a formal "black tie" concert, there are opportunities for effective staging which will enhance your presentations. For example,

- Bustling spirituals and show tunes seem to come alive when fingers are snapped or hands are clapped.
- Soloists add a dimension of drama when they enter from offstage while singing.
- Vocal sections can be moved into visual as well as musical relief through simple repositioning.

The easiest and quickest way to "block" positions and movements is by reviewing stage locations and body positions with your singers *before* giving

BASIC STAGE LOCATIONS

Up Right	Up Right Center	Up Center	Up Left Center	Up Left
Right	Right Center	Center	Left Center	Left
Down Right	Down Right Center	Down Center	Down Left Center	Down Left

AUDIENCE

Figure 12–1

them specific directions. Figure 12–1 presents the basic stage locations, and figure 12–2 shows traditional body positions in relation to the audience.

The following principles should be observed when planning for movement:

- Move with purpose
- Move in a straight line
- Avoid backward movement
- Keep still unless moving

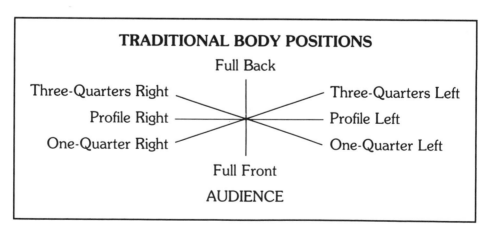

Figure 12–2

Appearance

Wardrobe requirements for a concert should be specified well in advance to provide singers time to "get their things in shape." Informing your choir boys that they will need black shoes two days later for the first church service, for example, may create an economic crisis for their families.

You may choose to provide a printed checklist in advance. If so, be very specific. I once told my college choir men to wear tuxedos. One of them showed up wearing a bright red shirt! Your list should include a reminder not to wear anything obtrusive such as polka dot socks, long dangling earrings, and hair glitter. Make sure your female singers avoid high heels. Some directors require a "dress inspection" well before a concert. If so, you should check for correctness, fit, and condition.

General conduct and deportment should also be discussed before the final rehearsal. Singers need to keep in mind that they represent their ensemble and should not engage in questionable social behavior which reflects negatively on the group. When backstage, they should keep a proper distance from equipment and crew and avoid making excessive noise.

The following guidelines should be presented when discussing stage deportment:

- Do not react or talk to individuals in the audience.
- All eyes on the conductor.
- If performing without music, keep arms and hands either at the side or in a specified position.
- Maintain proper posture throughout the performance.
- Look as though involved with the emotional content of the music.

Deportment should also be discussed with church singers. There must be general compliance with service rituals such as bowing in prayer and kneeling. Talking during the service should be avoided, and members need to sit still during the sermon or reading of the scripture.

Mental Preparation

For most choral performers, singing in a concert is an adventuresome experience requiring steady nerves. How can you prepare your singers psychologically for their concert? One obvious solution is to perform for any individuals willing to attend final rehearsals. Performing for other musicians is especially helpful since it motivates the ensemble to give their best. (See Situation 12–B.)

Another method is to make an audio tape recording of the choral group, then allow singers to evaluate their progress. Make sure, however, that you leave enough remaining rehearsal time to work out problems. Video recordings are especially useful for improving facial expression and developing physical poise. When used properly, recordings can build ensemble confidence.

SITUATION 12–B

Doris K. was preparing her college choir for an outdoor performance of show music. She recorded the piano accompaniment, then had her singers perform to the tape at lunch time outside the administration building. Within several minutes, a sizeable audience filled the courtyard.

Holding final rehearsals in a different location can also be beneficial. As singers adjust to new acoustics, they begin to listen and become more self-reliant.

COORDINATION OF MUSICAL ELEMENTS

Preparation of choral selections does not, in itself, guarantee a successful concert. How will the ensemble get its pitches? What steps will be necessary to combine the contributions of vocal soloists and instrumentalists most effectively? These are factors to be considered when you are coordinating musical elements.

Preparing Soloists

Vocal soloists require special attention by you. By working separately with them, you will save valuable ensemble rehearsal time. Even if a soloist is coached by a voice teacher, plan to spend enough time to at least work out problems of musical coordination and interpretation. (See Situation 12–C.) I find the following procedure to be effective:

1. As soon as soloists are chosen, let them know about musical decisions directly affecting their vocal part. Here are some specific examples:
   - Cuts

- Tempos
- Unusual changes, additions and deletions

2. Establish a deadline for soloists to be prepared to perform their music.

3. After this deadline, try to integrate the solos into regular rehearsals. This solves many coordination problems and allows both soloists and ensemble members to become more comfortable with the music.

4. Hold a solo rehearsal to establish your interpretive concepts, work out specific tempos, and coordinate musical cues.

SITUATION 12–C

Robert C. always seemed to have more than his share of church soloists. Several had never sung solos before joining the choir. One singer provided the answer: "He works with us until we know the music and have the confidence to do a good job."

Combining the Choral Ensemble With Instruments

Preparation for using instruments begins by using the full score in choral rehearsals to get used to the visual layout. As with vocal soloists, you must plan to hold at least one separate rehearsal with instrumentalists. Only in this way will you clearly hear and correct their problems. This also gives them a chance to find out how you intend to conduct the music. Then, when you hold the combined rehearsal, the instrumentalists will be in a better position to "carry the ball" if you need to devote part of your attention to the chorus.

Balance is the biggest potential problem you will face when you are working with singers and instrumentalists. The following remedies should be considered when the instrumental ensemble covers the choir:

1. Make sure that the choral group is elevated well above the instruments so that the vocal sound will project without interference.

2. If the singing is being "swallowed" by stage curtains, use sound deflectors or a shell.

3. Position instrumentalists so that their instruments point across stage rather than outwards toward the audience.

4. Shift all instrumental dynamic markings back one level whenever possible.

5. Consider positioning the chorus *alongside* of the instrumental ensemble. (See Figure 12–3.)

6. To ensure clarity of diction, have the singers explode their consonants.

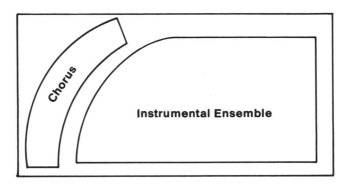

Figure 12–3

Preparing the Ensemble for Another Conductor

Occasionally, you may be faced with the task of preparing a vocal group for a performance conducted by someone else. The situation occurs most frequently when the orchestra or band director in a school is chosen to conduct a combined musical work. In order for this collaboration to be fruitful for all, you must avoid the following typical problems:

- The choir is not flexible enough to comply with the conductor's interpretation.
- Choral attacks and releases are vague or muddy.
- The ensemble is not sure where to come in after lengthy interludes.
- The singers cannot find locations where the director wishes to begin.

Preparation of the ensemble for another conductor must be considered as an *extra* step to be undertaken after the polishing and interpreting stage has been completed. The following requirements must be satisfied:

1. *Coordinate with the other conductor.* Find out if he or she plans to make cuts or alter the printed score in any way. Make sure that your vocal

group has the identical measure or rehearsal numbers as contained in the conductor's score.

2. *Overprepare your ensemble.* Take the necessary steps to ensure yourself that the choral group can perform the work correctly in spite of insufficient cues from the podium. For example, orchestra conductors do not usually pinpoint the treatment of consonants while conducting. Singers must be trained to do this independently.

If the work to be performed includes lengthy interludes, show the ensemble where to listen for musical cues occurring shortly before their entries. As a final test before turning the group over to the other conductor, see if the choir can perform its music with minimal direction.

3. *Develop flexibility.* Performing groups become so accustomed to their leader's way of doing things that they sometimes have difficulty adjusting to another conductor's interpretive ideas. You can facilitate this changeover by developing your singers' ability to perform the musical work with flexibility. During final rehearsals, change tempos, rallentandos, fermatas, and so on. Also, vary your conducting style wherever possible.

Giving Pitches

Special pitches or chords necessary to begin a choral work should be given as unobtrusively as possible during a concert. Generally speaking, it is a good idea to provide the choir with these tonal cues before the director comes on stage or during applause prior to the next selection. The mode chosen should be based on appropriate as well as on available sources. For example, do not select a trombone when a flute is on hand. Consider the following list of potential pitch sources.

- Pitch from within the ensemble by an individual with perfect pitch. Female voices carry the best.
- Pitch pipe played by someone within the choral group. This mode is less obtrusive than the choral director's use of a pitch pipe.
- Arpeggiated chord played lightly on the keyboard. I prefer the descending arpeggio because of its more buoyant effect.
- Pitch given by a treble instrument in the orchestra

CONCERT FACILITY ARRANGEMENTS

Performance halls are usually in heavy demand. This is especially true of school auditoriums, which may be used for everything from civic functions to study halls. Make sure that you book your ensemble as early as possible for necessary rehearsals on stage as well as for the actual concert. It is also a good idea to make these requests in writing. Many a concert has been jeopardized because of confused verbal commitments.

Choosing Technical Resources

As the concert date approaches, you should consider what available stage equipment and other physical resources will be needed to present your choral performance at its best. Use the following checklist in this planning:

1. Keyboard instruments
   a. Piano
      - Type
      - Condition
      - Stage location

   NOTE: Grand pianos are best placed centered in front of the ensemble. Uprights may also be centered without blocking the view by placing singers at each side of the piano.
   b. Organ
      - Location of console (lines of sight, moveable?)
      - Location of pipes or speakers (relationship to singers, moveable?)
2. Lighting
   a. For performers
      - Overhead lights sufficient for reading music
      - Music stand lights necessary for instrumentalists
   b. Special effects
      - Spotlights for soloists
      - Colored lighting for dramatic effect

   NOTE: Sophisticated lighting coordinated with musical selections will require preparation of a "light cue chart" for use by the stage crew.
3. Sound
   a. Acoustical
      - Reflectors or concert shell
      - Relation of singers to stage

   NOTE: Overhanging curtains tend to "swallow" sound when performers are placed too far upstage.

      b. Electronic
- Amplification needed for soloists, narrator, or ensemble
- Placement of microphones

  4. Physical requirements

      a. Risers
- Sufficient for group size
- Railings for safety

      b. Podium and conductor's stand

      c. Music stands for instrumentalists

      d. Stage curtains and backdrop

      e. Heating, cooling, and ventilation

Personnel Requirements

The next step is to determine what people will be required to move equipment, operate lights, hand out programs, and so on. In some cases, several of your own choir members will need to help out as ticket sellers or, in a pinch, even as stagehands. The important thing is to determine exactly what personnel will be needed, get as much support as possible from resources outside the singing organization, and then fill in the gaps with your own people where necessary. Here is a comprehensive list of possible personnel:

  1. House staff

      a. Ticket sellers who know prices and procedures

      b. Ushers in proper dress to take tickets, escort patrons to seats, hand out programs, and close auditorium doors

  2. Backstage

      a. Technicians to operate lights, sound system, and curtains

      b. Stagehands to move equipment on and off stage

  3. Custodial

      a. Security officers to unlock the facility

      b. Housekeeping staff to clean before and after concert

      NOTE: Don't forget a keyboard technician for tuning your piano.

CONDUCTING THE DRESS REHEARSAL

Directors usually devote the last rehearsal before a concert to a nonstop run-through of the entire program. There are advantages, however, to holding your "dress rehearsal" earlier, particularly if it will lessen undue last-minute fatigue.

This important rehearsal should take place at the concert facility so that proper tempos, balances, and dynamics can be determined, based on actual acoustics. Not to be overlooked are the nonmusical necessities which also need to be coordinated. I prefer to divide a dress rehearsal into three stages.

- Organization of nonmusical activities
- Coordination of light and sound
- Nonstop musical rehearsal

Organization of Nonmusical Activities

How will the ensemble line up and get onto stage? Where will soloists stand? These are typical problems which need to be resolved at dress rehearsal. An experienced choral group will have adopted certain procedures which do not need to be discussed or practiced at every final rehearsal. This is how I organize nonmusical activities for a new choir.

1. Form the ensemble in position on stage. Check for spacing and lines of sight. Designate which individuals will lead the choral group on and off stage.

2. Warm up the performers for later performance.

3. Clarify how music will be held while singers are moving and when to open choir folders.

4. Review guidelines for stage deportment.

5. Practice bowing. I ask singers to bow together at a prearranged signal, count silently to five, and then resume their attentive position. Soloists will also need guidelines at this point regarding movement into position and individual acknowledgement of applause.

6. Remind singers of prescribed concert dress, arrival time before the concert, and any other necessary points of information.

7. Practice all physical movements planned for the concert. This includes the initial entrance and final exit. Stress the need to move with purpose. Do not allow individuals to zigzag up the risers.

Coordination of Light and Sound

Lighting for a choral concert may vary from simple illumination of the stage to the elaborate use of spot and colored lights. In the latter case, an extra technical rehearsal may be required to position lights properly and coordinate special effects chosen to enhance the performance. When you are making decisions regarding lighting, do not overlook one fact—the performers must be able to see you *and* their printed music if it is being used in the concert. First make sure that the light level chosen to illuminate the stage is adequate. Then check to insure that any spotlights employed do not blind the singers.

One of the primary reasons for holding a dress rehearsal is to resolve possible problems of balance between performing forces. This is especially important when the final rehearsal represents the only opportunity for you to gather all performers on stage before the concert. Do not be impatient with this tedious task. It is better to be accused of being meticulous than to risk a performance tarnished by unheard soloists or a chorus inundated by its accompaniment. I utilize the following procedure when I am checking balances:

1. Rehearse musical sections performed by vocal soloists. If they are overpowered, move them as far forward as possible. If necessary, soften the accompaniment. As a last resort, consider audio amplification. Use this same approach for both instrumental and choral accompaniment.

2. Rehearse musical sections performed by individual vocal sections, female voices, and so on. Bring balances into line by modifying the volume levels of either the vocalists or their accompanying forces.

3. Rehearse the softest and then the loudest musical passages performed by the full ensemble. Make necessary adjustments.

Before plunging into the final stage of the dress rehearsal, you should determine your tempos for the works to be performed. Choose a representative passage or simply start at the beginning of each selection and experiment with several speeds until you find the ideal tempo for your acoustical conditions.

Nonstop Musical Rehearsal

The final segment of the dress rehearsal should be devoted to a complete, relatively uninterrupted performance of the choral program so that you and the singers can experience concert-like conditions. (See Situation 12–D.)

At this point, it is possible that some of your singers will begin to lose their "musical perspective." Some typical examples are:

- Too little contrast between dynamics
- Mumbled diction
- Tendency to sing note-to-note without regard for musical expression or flow
- Reverting to old, inferior tone quality

By giving verbal spot corrections without stopping performance, you can help to alleviate these types of "stage fright" problems.

SITUATION 12–D

Rosemary F. was highly recommended for her first high school choral position, yet the principal complained of mediocre concerts and low ratings in annual competitions. Her singers complained that she treated dress rehearsals just like any other rehearsal. Consequently, they were unable to bridge the gap from rehearsal to concert performance.

Occasionally, it may be necessary to modify the program order at a dress rehearsal when instrumentalists are to be used. It may be best to rehearse the selections they play all at one time and schedule them for part of the rehearsal to avoid wasting their time.

PRE-CONCERT ACTIVITIES

Prior to the actual concert, the ensemble should gather for warm-up exercises and for reviewing critical musical sections in the repetoire. The director should arrive before the singers to make sure that things are in order for the concert. Following is a comprehensive checklist for a full-scale concert involving a sizeable support staff.

1. Auditorium
   - Unlocked
   - Lighted
   - Proper temperature
   - Clean
   - Flowers

2. Stage
   - Risers
   - Chairs
   - Podium
   - Conductor's stand
   - Instrumentalists' chairs and stands
   - Sound reflectors
   - Piano, other keyboards
   - Lighting
   - Curtains and backdrops
   - Props
3. Backstage
   - Meeting and changing rooms unlocked
   - Security for valuables
   - Chairs for performers to relax in while waiting
   - Stage crew present
4. Lobby
   - Tickets and sellers
   - Programs and ushers

Pre-concert activities may be held on stage. However, this often results in a rush to get through the music before the audience arrives. It is better to choose a spacious meeting place out of earshot from the concert hall.

Because this last-minute meeting is so important to the success of the performance, insist that all performers arrive punctually at the designated location. Welcome your singers when they arrive and set them at ease. This is especially important for young soloists.

I prefer to call a relatively early meeting time and get a good start on pre-concert activities. This allows the performers time for mental preparation before the concert, and a few minutes to tidy up.

Consider the following suggestions when you are planning and conducting final pre-concert activities:

1. Before arriving, locate specific places in the music that you wish to rehearse. Note on an index card their locations and what you expect to achieve.

2. Write down on another index card important last-minute reminders you want to announce to your choir.

3. Emphasize mental alertness when you are warming up the ensemble and reviewing music.

4. Accentuate the positive; eliminate the negative.

MINIMIZING PERFORMANCE ERRORS

It is understandable why choral directors sometimes feel as if they are "at the mercy of the gods" once a concert gets underway. With so many human beings involved, there is always the possibility of mishap. Actually there are several things we can do to control the outcome of a performance without interfering with the audience's enjoyment. Two courses of action are available:

- Develop concert sign language
- Maintain mental alertness

Develop Concert Sign Language

Several specific gestures can be worked out between you and your singers to be used when problems arise in performance. These signs should be as unobtrusive as possible. Here is a list of gestures I have found to be useful.

- Left hand finger pointed upward to raise pitch
- Finger pointed downward to control sharping
- Elevate palm upward to keep music folders at proper height
- Point at self while aligning body to improve posture
- Open and close mouth to maintain singing with dropped jaws

Maintain Mental Alertness

Most mistakes occurring in performance can be directly attributed to lack of concentration. One way to overcome this insidious problem is by reminding all to observe the following rule:

As the concert lengthens, concentrate more.

During performance there are little things you can do to keep the ensemble members alert. If I notice an individual "going off on another wave length," I may deliberately make a face to regain the singer's attention. Sometimes it even pays to whisper something funny between selections or to make an awkward gesture just to keep the group loose and on its toes.

Make sure that you yourself do not fall victim to inattentiveness. Be especially careful for the following:

- Critical cues
- Surprise changes in meter
- Sudden dynamics at page turns
- Important tempo changes

Always strive to stay on top of every concert situation. For example, by thinking ahead, you will remember to acknowledge soloists and accompanists for audience applause.

CHAPTER 13

EVALUATING THE CHORAL PROGRAM AND ITS PARTICIPANTS

Choral directors tend to be "results-oriented" people. And one obvious way to claim a successful choral program is by presenting superior performances. Sometimes, however, this kind of goal orientation can result in a "winning-at-any-cost" philosophy. (See Situation 13–A.) Consequently values such as nurturing vocal growth, developing musical understanding, or providing for aesthetic response to a rich variety of repertoire may be entirely overlooked.

SITUATION 13–A

Thomas M's high school ensembles usually took top honors in competitions. But his graduating singers earned a reputation among college choral directors as being rigid and intolerant of other views about vocal techniques. A visit to the high school director's rehearsals provided the answer: he was autocratic and intimidating.

ASSESSING THE PROGRAM

There are many aspects to consider when attempting to evaluate your entire choral program. For example, Robert Sidnell suggests that the following areas should be evaluated in various kinds of music programs:[1]

1. Philosophy of the program
2. Terminal goals
3. Course division and program objectives
4. Content, sequence, and instructional objectives
5. Nature of learning experiences
6. Scheduling and facilities

---

[1]Robert Sidnell, *Building Instructional Programs in Music Education* (Englewood Cliffs: Prentice-Hall, 1973), p. 136.

If applied to your choral program, whether it be school, church, or community-oriented, Sidnell's criteria can be lumped into three large categories.

- Long-range review
- Intermediate evaluation
- Daily assessment

Long-Range Review

Have you ever found yourself questioning the value of your choral program? This kind of "reflective evaluation" is essential if we are to avoid being caught up in the "nitty-gritty" day-to-day routine of things. By stepping back, we can look at our program as a whole. A long-range review should be undertaken at the end of each choral year.

A successful business consultant recently offered me several criteria he uses when evaluating corporations.

1. *Mission, goals, and purpose.* Does your ensemble fulfill an honest, essential role in the school, church, or community? Has its purpose been defined? Are its goals achieved directly or in a roundabout way? Are the singers' personal interests compatible with the group's mission?

    In Chapter 2 the following areas of development were deemed necessary for a well-balanced program:
    - Vocal skills
    - Musical knowledge
    - Musicianship
    - Ensemble
    - Social skills

    Do you emphasize or exclude any of these areas?

2. *Quality of the product.* With the exception of professional choirs, it is not always essential that you demand absolute perfection as a standard for performance quality. It *is* essential, however, that your vocal group strive for realistic goals. For a small country church choir, this might mean conveying a simple anthem with textual clarity, spiritual feeling, and musical integrity.

    Is the level of quality appropriate for your ensemble? Are your standards compatible with the singers' limitations or aspirations? Do your *rehearsals* offer qualitative experiences for members? Are your performances imbued with a quality of spirit and enthusiasm?

3. *Organizational direction.* Is the ensemble "heading in the right direction"? Are there signs of growth and development? Or is the group "standing still in the water"?

   Singers' attitudes usually serve as a barometer for the group's overall sense of direction and achievement. Are they excited about upcoming performances? Do they commit themselves to excellence? Perhaps trends in membership need to be examined. Do you have more or fewer performers this year?

4. *Image.* Does your ensemble receive accurate and ample recognition for its ability? Does it "draw a good crowd" for its concerts?

   Sometimes community vocal organizations go unnoticed by the public because of inadequate marketing. Do you "sell" your school choral program by letting others know you had a successful off-campus tour?

5. *Service.* What outside needs are serviced by your choir? Does it tour as an ambassador for the school or perform benefit concerts for worthy causes? How about having those church choir members split into quartets after a Christmas season rehearsal, then traveling to invalids and caroling to them?

Intermediate Evaluation

This level of assessment is best undertaken after a rehearsal-concert period has been completed. For church choir directors the respite immediately after Christmas and Easter is a good time to reflect on events past.

In conducting this mid-level evaluation, I like to review, in reverse order, major events as they occurred. Some essential "milestones" to consider are:

1. Concerts
   * Quality of performance
   * Audience size
   * Audience response to repertoire
   * Concert facilities
   * House staff and procedures
2. Dress Rehearsal
   * Coordination of musical elements
   * Coordination of sight, sound, and group movement
   * Achievement of final preparation

3. Daily Rehearsals
   • Achievement of musical and nonmusical goals
   • Sense of purpose and motivation
   • Rehearsal facility
   • Rehearsal activities and procedures
4. Initial Rehearsals
   • Establishment of standard operating procedures
   • Dissemination of music
   • Coordination with accompanist

Daily Assessment

Day-to-day evaluation is concerned primarily with individual rehearsals. Before discussing criteria to be examined, it is important to understand the dynamic process which typically occurs within the rehearsal.

• The director "brings" to the rehearsal preparation and planning.
• The singer "brings" to the rehearsal a willingness to participate and achieve.
• For success to occur, communication, teaching, and learning must take place.
• Results are enhanced by motivation and rapport.

This dynamic process is illustrated in Figure 13–1.

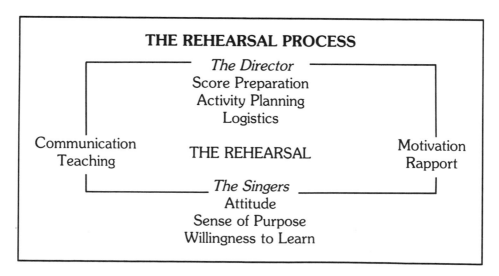

Figure 13–1

By keeping this fundamental process in mind when evaluating rehearsals, problems and solutions become clarified. For example, if thorough planning and presentation by the director result in a mediocre rehearsal, the problem may be traced to the singers' attitude or lack of support.

The next step in the daily evaluation process is to examine in detail each of the criteria mentioned.

1. *Planning.* Was your initial concept suitable for reaching rehearsal objectives? Did you anticipate problems with viable solutions?

2. *Implementation.* Did you choose appropriate teaching strategies? Were they presented in logical sequence?

3. *Motivation.* Were students enthusiastic about reaching goals? Did they rehearse with a sense of achievement and purpose?

4. *Communication.* Did the singers understand your intentions? Are they informed about procedures and future events?

5. *Logistics.* Is music distributed and identified with efficiency? Are those "physical things" like heating and tuned pianos taken care of?

Quite often a problematic rehearsal can be traced directly to your Daily Rehearsal Plan. In Chapter 6, a format based on sequence of activities, repertoire, and strategies was presented. If you are having music-learning difficulties, perhaps some of your objectives are unrealistic. If unusual vocal problems are occurring, maybe the repertoire is too difficult or your vocal exercises are inadequate.

CHORAL DIRECTING DEMANDS CONTINUAL ASSESSMENT

Unlike dead-end jobs, which often force individuals to repeat a small repertoire of skills, choral directing requires diversification and growth. Even in choral situations hampered by such restrictions as an insensitive administration or limited funds, the enterprising director will usually find ways to build a quality choral program. It is safe to assume that almost all top-notch vocal organizations got that way despite their inadequacies and because of dynamic leadership.

As obvious as it may seem, it is easy to forget that the first step necessary to solve a problem is to recognize that the problem does, in fact, exist. For choral directors this means honestly assessing our repertoire of skills and knowledge for weaknesses and "rust spots." Here are two factors to keep in mind:

- There is a big difference between prerequisite qualification and real effectiveness. Beginning choral directors who have received training in basic conducting skills can be compared with young army officers —they are equipped merely to survive the battle.

- Growth is continuous, but it requires the sacrifice of sedateness. On the other hand, development is an essential component of true professionalism.

Evaluating Musical Skills and Knowledge

Besides conducting with facility, you must learn to manage an array of associated but integral musical skills and knowledge. These musical "components" can be classified according to their type of activity and their level of difficulty. The Taxonomy of Choral Skills and Knowledge represents a highly systematized classification of these musical responsibilities. If you will rate your ability for each subcategory, strengths and deficiencies will become immediately apparent. The following taxonomy is a unique guide for self-improvement.

I. SKILLS

In each of the following five skill categories, rate yourself on each skill as follows: cannot perform, poor, fair, good, or excellent.

A. SINGING
   Subcategories
   1. Sing in tune
   2. Sing with tonal control
   3. Sing with technical proficiency
   4. Sing with stylistic diversification
   5. Sing with musical expression

B. VOCAL SIGHT READING
   Subcategories
   1. Sing own vocal line
   2. Sing various vocal lines in treble and bass clefs
   3. Sing individual lines in keyboard accompaniment
   4. Sing individual instrumental lines in various clefs

C. KEYBOARD PLAYING
   Subcategories
   1. Accompany warm-up exercises
   2. Play individual vocal lines in treble and bass clefs
   3. Play combined vocal lines in closed score
   4. Play combined vocal lines in open score
   5. Play keyboard accompaniment for score study
   6. Play keyboard accompaniment in rehearsals
   7. Play keyboard accompaniment in performances
   8. Play combined instrumental lines in open score

D. LISTENING
   Subcategories
   1. Hear faulty intonation
   2. Hear incorrect notes in melodic line
   3. Hear incorrect notes within harmonic structure
   4. Hear incorrect dynamic levels
   5. Hear faulty phrasing
   6. Hear improper blend
   7. Hear improper balance
   8. Hear incorrect articulation

E. RHYTHMIC PERCEPTION
   Subcategories
   1. Choose proper tempos
   2. Maintain steady tempos
   3. Hear incorrect rhythms
   4. Sense underlying pulsation and stress
   5. Have feel for rhythmic deviations such as syncopation and hemiola

F. DICTION
   Subcategories
   1. Pronounce English texts with precision
   2. Pronounce foreign texts with precision
   3. Detect inaccuracies in ensemble diction
   4. Translate foreign texts for essential meaning

G. SILENT SCORE STUDY
   Subcategories

   1. Hear individual vocal lines
   2. Hear combined vocal lines
   3. Hear keyboard accompaniment
   4. Hear combined instrumental lines
   5. Hear harmonic progressions and key changes

II. KNOWLEDGE

In each of the following five knowledge categories rate yourself in each area as follows: do not know, poor, fair, good, or excellent.

A. TERMINOLOGY AND SYMBOLS
   Subcategories

   1. Know terms and symbols for tempos
   2. Know terms and symbols for dynamics
   3. Know expressive terms and symbols
   4. Know articulation terms and symbols
   5. Know designations and abbreviations for instruments

B. SCORE MECHANICS
   Subcategories

   1. Understand directions for movement through the score (repeats, endings)
   2. Know usual locations of choral parts and instrumental families within score
   3. Know intervals of transposition for pertinent instruments

C. THEORETICAL INSIGHT
   Subcategories

   1. Locate keys (or tonal structure) and modulations
   2. Analyze form
   3. Locate melodic, harmonic, and rhythmic tension and release
   4. Identify characteristics which give the work its specific identity

D. CHORAL HISTORY AND REPERTOIRE
   Subcategories

   1. Understand relative importance of composers in perspective

2. Know their choral works

3. Know quality works by lesser known composers

4. Have grasp of choral repertoire in various stylistic periods, for various accompanying forces, and for various types of choral ensembles

E. PERFORMANCE PRACTICE
   Subcategories

1. Know the expressive possibilities of various types of voices

2. Know the expressive possibilities and limitations of the various instruments, including organ

3. Understand basic concepts and traditions for performing music from all stylistic periods

Pursuing Avenues of Growth

Various nonmusical roles are necessary for choral directors. Obviously if these duties were broken down into general skills and knowledge and added to the Taxonomy of Choral Skills and Knowledge, we would have an impressive checklist of things to do throughout our choral directing lifetime.

The question is: how can we begin to satisfy these professional requirements? The answer is: by pursuing three main avenues of learning and experience:

- *Self-accumulated skills and knowledge.* This is gradually accomplished through individual practice and direct access to information in books and other reference materials.

- *Guidance and consultation.* Other choral directors, teachers, and nonmusical specialists are sought for needed improvement, clarification, and further information.

- *Performance opportunities.* General musicianship as well as conducting skills are sharpened through individual, chamber, and larger ensemble performing experiences. This also includes music making outside of the choral field.

Here are three concrete ways to pursue these avenues of growth:

1. *Attend workshops, conventions, and courses.* Competent choral directors actively seek help from others. Workshops and conventions are

typical avenues for improvement. For example, the American Choral Directors Association sponsors state workshops as well as district and national conventions. Activities include specific topic sessions led by reputable choral specialists and concerts performed by excellent ensembles. Often much insight develops out of informal "rap sessions" between directors talking shop during their leisure.

Colleges and universities have come a long way in offering more specialized courses for the established choral director. What conductor would not benefit by seeing an instant replay of his or her technique on videotape or by taking a refresher course in choral repertoire? Not to be overlooked are courses in such areas as social psychology and management.

2. *Attend concerts.* The choral director who does not find the time to attend concerts endangers all chances of growth, for only through attending concerts can we begin to see our own efforts in perspective. Besides hearing new repertoire, the visiting director can compare interpretations, methods of programming, and quality of ensemble response.

Attending nonchoral performances by professional musicians is also important, primarily because these concerts help to provide general standards of quality and aesthetic inspiration. Here are two suggestions which I have found to be personally useful:
   - Attend rehearsals as well as performances and sit close to the director. You will learn much about gesture, communication, and working rapport.
   - Watch televised presentations of major orchestra concerts on the public television channel. Camera coverage of these performances provides unique views of world-renowned conductors.

3. *Perform.* It is unfortunate that some choral directors become numbed to music's expressive qualities because they have partially lost contact with their own art. Personal involvement in active music making, aside from conducting, is the best defense against musical insensitivity. There are two available avenues of performance, each providing separate rewards.
   a. Performing as a soloist will help you to sharpen your talents, abilities, and overall musicianship. The process of preparing for a recital also has many correlations with group preparation.
   b. Singing in a choral ensemble may sound like a "busman's holiday," but it provides you the opportunity to re-experience the problems

and responsibilities which your choristers encounter. In better choral groups it also offers the chance to experience interdependence between vocal and accompanying forces. There are also two secondary reasons for performing in choral ensembles:

- Proficiency in score reading is developed.
- Other directors are observed "under fire."

Broadening Perspective

Continual growth as a choral director requires keeping up with a wide range of new ideas and innovations. Here are some examples:

- New music
- Early period music published in performance editions for the first time
- Techniques for teaching contemporary music
- Concepts for improving diction and tone quality
- New audio-visual aids

Growth also means dynamic movement from a grasp of basic choral skills to more general musical competencies. For example, understanding music history will give you a perspective about composers and a sense of direction in looking for repertoire. Have you ever heard of Luca Marenzio or Giacomo Gastoldi? These Renaissance musicians produced fine choral works, and their music is readily available.

Finally, growth means improvement in nonmusical tasks and activities. Finding better ways to work with people who sing and learning to organize one's own administrative functions more efficiently are prime examples. (See Situation 13–B.)

SITUATION 13–B

Susan W. received a flattering compliment from one of her singers. The choir member informed her that she was especially appreciated by the ensemble because she "cared for them" and because she "had interests in other areas besides music."

EVALUATING AND TESTING SINGERS

Successful leaders continually assess their groups. A simple glance at the eyes of her students may reveal to the college professor how ready they are for learning. The boy scouts were required to demonstrate skills in bandaging and pass a written test before receiving their first aid merit badge from the troop leader.

Informal Evaluation

Choral groups are comprised of singers with varying interests, values, abilities, and experiences. Seasoned directors have learned they cannot view individuals indifferently as "cogs in a wheel." We must continually evaluate our singers so that we may help them. Some areas to observe are:

1. *Attendance.* Does the singer attend regularly? Is lateness a problem? Are there conflicts with home or other organizations?

2. *Participation.* Is the singer a "willing learner?" Is there enthusiasm? Does he or she offer suggestions and respond to questions?

3. *Vocal performance.* Does the individual appear to be comfortable with the assigned vocal part? Are there signs of tension? Is the singer a "vocal leader," a "good blender," or a detriment to sectional quality?

4. *Musicianship.* Are notes learned rapidly? Is the singer a good memorizer? Are interpretive concepts comprehended and retained?

5. *Personal.* Does the individual "fit into the group"? Are there unusual or excessive personal problems?

If problems are encountered, you must be prepared to offer individualized attention. Problems involving attendance, participation, and those of a personal nature are best remedied through a one-on-one meeting with the singer. Vocal problems can often be eliminated or minimalized by mini-lessons. More extensive musicianship problems may require additional coaching sessions or music courses.

Grading

Singers in school vocal ensembles often receive grades for participation. The question of what kind of grades to give or how to determine them are controversial issues. Two major opposing views can be summarized as follows:

- *Pro:* Certain singers "carry the load" more than others and should be rewarded accordingly. Furthermore, there are important areas of growth in musical skills and knowledge which should be evaluated.

- *Con:* If a good choral director motivates all to do their best and if ensemble performance is excellent, then every singer deserves a high grade.

Another problem confusing the issue is whether to grade for talent or effort. A less talented singer may have difficulty earning a high grade despite significant effort. One solution is to offer grades on a pass/fail basis, eliminating the need to determine whether an individual deserves a grade for average, good, or excellent work and ability.

Many directors employ the following formula in assigning letter grades:

The final grade is determined by averaging individual grades for each of the following categories:

Attendance
  A = Perfect
  B = Good
  C = Fair
  D = Poor

Vocal performance
  A = Leadership
  B = Positive
  C = Neutral
  D = Detrimental

Participation
  A = Enthusiastic
  B = Active
  C = Passive
  D = Uncooperative

This approach allows for grading without detracting from rehearsal time. Its biggest drawback is that it does not include objective testing. Here are some types of tests you can use to evaluate your singers during rehearsal periods.

1. *Music learning.* Form random quartets from your ensemble and have them perform short musical sections. Grade them for rhythmic and pitch accuracy.

2. *Memorization.* Request one row of a vocal section to perform a part from memory. Walk in front of them and listen for memory lapses.

3. *Knowledge.* Give short musical quizzes based on musical symbols and terminology.

4. *Musicianship.* Have a few individuals sing their vocal part against piano accompaniment. Grade them for diction, phrasing, and interpretation.

INDEX